"Vital Signs is a powerful, much needed book which raises a very real question. Are Christians armed for the struggle against the many social forces that undermine faith? The authors make sophisticated use of survey data in spelling out the many problems that confront sincere Christians and offer new approaches that ought to be carefully considered by both clergy and laity. In my opinion their book is right on the mark."

George Gallup, Jr.
President of the Gallup Poll

Vital Signs

*Emerging Social Trends and the
Future of American Christianity*

GEORGE BARNA
WILLIAM PAUL McKAY

CROSSWAY BOOKS • WESTCHESTER, ILLINOIS
A DIVISION OF GOOD NEWS PUBLISHERS

Vital Signs. Copyright © 1984 by George Barna and William Paul McKay. Published by Crossway Books, a division of Good News Publishers, Westchester, Illinois 60153.

First printing, 1984

Printed in the United States of America

Library of Congress Catalog Card Number 84-70658

ISBN 0-89107-312-4 (Paperback)
ISBN-0-89107-324-8 (Cloth)

Contents

v

Acknowledgments

Few research-based pieces of literature can accurately be thought of as self-contained. Various external forms of creativity, insight, and assistance invariably influence the final product. This book is no different.

The accumulation of statistics and other information is a taxing, laborious process. Such efforts are especially significant in a book about social trends. Gregg Quiggle deserves a tremendous amount of credit for his diligence and savvy in discovering and obtaining much of the information that is contained in this work. His enduring interest in the project and its potential is genuinely appreciated.

The authors, who operate American Resource Bureau of Wheaton, relied heavily upon survey data collected by the company since 1979. Without the consistent, reliable work of members of the research staff, much of the information in this book would not have been acquired. We have been blessed with many high-quality telephone interviewers. The supervisory efforts of Don Phelps and Larry Reid deserve mention. Many a prayer of thanks has been lifted up on behalf of the thousands of individuals who allowed us to interrupt their evenings to provide information on how they live, what they believe, what motivates them to act, etc.

A number of our colleagues in the Christian community have generously given of their time, expertise, and enthusiasm by critiquing drafts, providing ideas, or supplying hard-to-get information. We extend our warm gratitude and appreciation to Harvey Bostrom, Bill Hybels, Tom Ivy, Jim Johnson, John Mallory, Marjorie McKay, Paul Robbins, John Tofilon, and John Whitehead.

George Gallup, Jr. has earned our unflagging respect and admiration for his willingness to share information and lend his insight to this project. In an era when most businessmen are devoted to stifling their competition, George's hospitality and kindness was a tribute to his commitment to the furtherance of the Kingdom of God, rather than the stockpiling of earthly treasures. We pray that our response to people who consult us in the future will be as loving and helpful.

Managing details, typing and retyping drafts, fending off intrusions—this and much more was done for us by our assistants, Linda Leedom and Darla Scheidt. Their dedication and professionalism played a significant role in the timely completion of this book.

Crossway Books, through the efforts of Jan and Lane Dennis, deserves credit for capturing our vision for this project, and helping us in the thematic development and editorial process. We have learned much from them throughout this endeavor, and are grateful that their sense of spiritual duty always transcended the hard-core business end of the process. Working with them has been a pleasure.

Last, but never least, are our wives, Nancy Barna and Janet McKay. Undoubtedly, their advice to the unsuspecting would be, "never marry someone who wants to write a book." These two gems have been subjected to endless drafts and rewrites, endless conversations about the topics encompassed in the book, and endless complaints about "writer's block," "burnout," and "creative frustration." We praise God that their endurance and love for us and our work were also endless. This book is dedicated to these two women, who sacrificed so much of their own lives for the life of this project. May any glory that results from the book go to God; and may the resulting satisfaction that it was worth the price go to Nancy and Jan.

Lest the fingers of blame point astray, the authors alone are responsible for any flaws in logic and information that appear in this book.

George Barna
William Paul McKay

1 Social Transformation: The Challenge to Christianity in America

This is a book about the future. More specifically, it is the story of America's born-again Christian population as it approaches a crossroad.[1]

Futurists and social analysts are in agreement that this country has entered a period of radical social change. The very foundation upon which our culture has been based is being fundamentally altered. Because of the "ripple effect" of change—whereby even very small modifications of one part of society affect all other parts of society—the Christian population of this nation is being significantly affected by the social metamorphosis that is underway. The purpose of this book is to evaluate how Christians are responding to the changes that have already started to reshape the contours of American society.

John Naisbitt, Alvin Toffler, and other cultural observers have provided a well-documented, detailed vision of the United States' future.[2] By all indicators, the America we knew in 1980 will bear scant resemblance to the America we will experience in 1990. The economic character of the nation will shift from an industrial base to an information-oriented economy; the processing of raw materials will be replaced by the processing of ideas, facts, data. Technological developments—many of which will be associated with computer advances—will redefine the skills required in the job market.

The loneliness, alienation, and lack of fulfillment that characterized the seventies and early eighties will be checked by scaled-down institutions and social systems that encourage individual participation and personal involvement. Mass society will succumb to a localized, personalized culture.

Even the distribution of the population will change. The pattern of family mobility begun in the late seventies—in which millions of people fled the Northeast and Midwest in favor of the warm, opportunity-laden South and Far West—will gain momentum. The traditional power bases and resource centers will be relocated in the process.

Foundational values, beliefs, and attitudes will undergo the harsh scrutiny of a public struggling to attain a sense of purpose and identity. The unprecedented rate of change that will reshape this nation will render such scrutiny a matter of survival rather than intellectual curiosity. A new perspective on life, unrestrained by the traditions and assumptions of the past, will emerge. As researcher Daniel Yankelovich has cautioned, "American civilization will never be the same."[3]

But what about the fifty million adults whose primary allegiance is not to a "civil religion," or to "the American dream," but to Jesus Christ? Will born-again Christians ignore the spiritual implications of the social revolution and go along with the crowd? Will Christians understand the challenge the present cultural upheaval presents to the survival of their spiritual heritage and purpose?

In the chapters that follow, data from national public opinion surveys and behavioral research studies will explore the reactions of born-again Christians to the early manifestations of social change, and will discuss the responses most likely to occur in the future. Although the absolute survival of Christianity is not in question, its capacity to affect society will be severely challenged. The indications are that Christians are not sufficiently armed for the struggle. The signs of the impending collapse, which the succeeding chapters will examine in fuller detail, include the following:

- Despite widespread agreement among Christians that divorce is detrimental to the family and its individual members (as well as being antithetical to the biblical position on marriage), born-again individuals are every bit as likely as nonbelievers to have suffered the agony of a broken marriage. There are some ten million Christians in the U.S. who have experienced divorce.

- Although abortion has traditionally been viewed as a rallying issue for the born-again community, surveys indicate that over the past several years their attitudes on this subject have become increasingly liberal.

- By and large Christians are politically illiterate. Despite heightened awareness in some issue areas, the majority of Christians remain inactive and unconcerned about policy developments.

- Churches have failed to provide members with strong, effective leadership in worship, personal spiritual growth, private counseling, and the development of community.

- The spiritual walk of Christian individuals has been retarded by their frequent, if unconscious, support of philosophies and activities contradictory to the Christian perspective. The most obvious failings relate to the acceptance of materialism, hedonism, and secular humanism.

- Despite the millions of dollars spent on media ministry and evangelistic publishing, there has been no real growth in the size of the Christian population in the past five years.

- Some conflict still remains between Protestants and Catholics over which group is truly Christian. While Protestants typically perceive their tradition to be the only source of born-again believers, Catholics actually represent the second largest denominational affiliate of those who claim to be born again. Ignorant of this fact, Protestants have unwittingly isolated themselves from many Catholics through their overt hostility.

These factors, when combined with other, similarly distressing indications, raise some serious questions as to the fate of Christianity in coming decades. There are traces of hope to be found, as in the rapidly spreading revolt against secularized education, or concerning the creative zeal with which some Christian media ministries are approaching new communications technologies. However, even in those areas serious obstacles must be overcome. It could certainly be argued that any impact that Christianity is having on American culture is largely happening by God's grace—in spite of his people, not because of them.

The pages that follow are an attempt to present an objective analysis of the current condition and likely prospects for Christianity in America through the end of this decade. The reality is that the integrity of the Christian faith is being severely tested by a social transformation of massive proportions. All available evidence indicates a body of believers unprepared to meet the challenge. The hour is getting very late. If the Christian community is to remain faithful to the life-transforming gospel witness, it must find ways to resist the corrosive influences of godless humanism that have affected it so greatly already and to grasp the opportunities for renewal that change often brings with it.

Will Christians be equal to the challenge? We don't know. But an awareness of where we are now and where we apparently are going is essential. That awareness is what we hope to provide in this book.

2 The American Family Under Change

Television producer Norman Lear, a political liberal and champion of the secular humanist school of thought, has suggested that many American fathers and husbands look, think, and speak like Archie Bunker. At the other end of the spectrum is evangelist Jerry Falwell, a standard-bearer of the political right and a fundamentalist Christian. Falwell has adamantly defended the traditional home in which the father is primarily responsible for both the economic and spiritual well-being of the family, while the mother tends to the welfare of her husband and children. There are, of course, numerous gradations between these two extremes. People as diverse as feminist leader Gloria Steinem, ERA opponent Phyllis Schlafly, Senator Paul Laxalt, and even television talk show host Phil Donahue have significantly influenced the future, if not the very structure, of the American household.

A large number of born-again Christians are caught in the maelstrom of conflicting beliefs about the family. They see the need for change in certain traditional concepts, but find it impossible to embrace some of the liberal perspectives about family that violate their understanding of Christian values.

The social and economic changes that will reshape America during the next two decades could well unravel 6,000 years of basic family traditions. Household leadership, home economics, sexual attitudes, child-rearing practices, and marital arrangements are some of the vital areas that will be dramatically affected. The ultimate destiny of the family as we know it may be determined by the outcome of what some have called "the world's greatest sociological experiment"—America's testing of the family unit.

This is no casual experiment; the stakes are high. Judging by its deeds, America is willing to take the risk of radically altering the established nature of the family. The widespread demand for greater personal fulfillment during this time of economic turbulence has set in motion forces that might lead to a more advanced state of civilization—or to social disaster. Will we achieve a synthesis of traditional commitments and new forms of fulfillment, thus creating a new direction for society? Or will we end up with the worse of two worlds—a society fragmented and anomic? Will the family be in shambles? Will the work ethic collapse? Will our code of morals and ethics be spineless and self-centered? Will personal freedom be eroded? Indeed, the tensions emanating from our experimentation with the family could result in an era of bitter and divisive social conflict. Is America ready and able to pay the price should this grand experiment fail?

Historical Context

Dialectical tensions, although imperceptible to most people, have been at work on the traditional family since the close of the last world war. One of those tensions has risen from individuals' unbridled passion for the material benefits made possible by the successful industrialization of this nation. The acquisition of automobiles, larger homes, electronic gadgets, and opportunities for travel have become the working definition of the "pursuit of happiness." For the first time in history we have a middle class whose accumulation of wealth is comparable to that of the world's historic elite.

The range of social and economic options available to the post-World War II family has been unparalleled. With Social Security and Medicare programs in full operation, for the first time many families were able to place their aged parents in specially designed care centers. Meanwhile, many women chose to augment their family earnings, thereby increasing their disposable income and the number of "pleasure options" open to them. Education played an increasingly important role in the lives of young people, becoming the most convenient avenue toward achievement of the American dream.

Then suddenly, as might happen in a horror movie, ominous forces—such as OPEC, runaway inflation, and the nuclear arms race—seemed to arise from nowhere to challenge the mighty United States' economic foundation. Words like *inflation* crept into the vocabulary of the average person. Increases in the cost of living eliminated the disposable income of many families. Savings accounts dwindled as families tried to cope with increases in taxes, college expenses, food, and medical bills. Women who had chosen to work for a little extra money, or to break the monotony of their household routine, became chained to the work force.

The events of the seventies intensified the problems. The value of the dollar sank to new lows. American industry lost its competitive edge in the international market, and productivity rates declined. As social analyst Daniel Yankelovich noted, "In a matter of a few years, we have moved from an uptight culture set in a dynamic economy to a dynamic culture set in an uptight economy."[1]

Along with the economic disruptions came a series of shock waves that rattled the foundations of the social order. Many American families proved to be incapable of coping with the mounting tensions. The "generation gap" widened with each new demand for social change by American youth. The family itself began to shift from its traditional form to an institution that reflected the underlying motives of the "me generation." Homosexual relationships gained acceptance. Abortions became readily available and increasingly popular. The divorce rate climbed off the charts.

The effects of this culture revolution were keenly felt in the Christian community as well. Christians have traditionally embraced a belief in the sacredness of marriage. The social tensions that have emerged since the midsixties, however, have instigated rapid transformations in the attitudes of many Christians toward divorce.

Divorce: The Tension of Breaking Away

Just after the turn of the century, in 1910, only one-tenth of one percent of the nation's population (83,000 people) had experienced divorce.[2] Times have changed. In 1982 alone, 1.18 million couples saw their marriages dissolve.[3] The steep and consistent incline of the trend line in the accompanying graph illustrates the increasing acceptance of divorce as an option in problem marriages. As time marches on, Americans are more and more willing to experiment and to search for alternatives to unsatisfactory marriages.

At this critical juncture, even the Christian home is feeling the impact of divorce. In 1983 there were ten million born-again Christians who had been divorced at one point in their lives. Marital separation—a step that almost inevitably leads to formal divorce—characterized the lives of an additional one million Christian families.[4]

The problem of divorce has not been confined to the "average" Christian home. In an article in *Christianity Today* entitled "Clergy Divorce Spills into the Aisle," one scholar suggested that the divorce rate among ministers has more than quadrupled since 1960.[5] The numbing effect and consequent indifference of Christians toward clergy divorce is clearly demonstrated by the slight reaction of the Christian community to the recent divorce of the son of a well-known, highly visible television evangelist. One day the evangelist's son and his wife were on screen singing and testifying to the love of Christ. Just days later, without fanfare or explanation, the son appeared on the program and introduced his new partner for life and ministry. Apparently impervious to the incident, that ministry has continued to reap solid financial support and maintains a weekly viewership of several million people. With increasing frequency, laymen are able to point to the shattered marriage of their pastor in an attempt to justify their own marital breakups.

Table 2.1

**Christian vs. Non-Christian Attitudes
Towards Divorce**

Statement	Christians	Non-Christians
Divorce is never acceptable.	4%	4%
Divorce is justifiable only in a few unusual cases.	31%	14%
Divorce is an acceptable solution if the couple has tried to work out their problems but failed to do so.	61%	69%
Divorce is a good solution to problem marriages and should not be discouraged.	2%	9%

A study of the attitudes of Christians shows just how far the pendulum has swung away from the traditional perception of the marriage bond. One national opinion survey, conducted by American Resource Bureau in December of 1983, asked people to choose one of four statements to describe their feelings about divorce. Segregating the responses of Christians from those of non-Christians showed surprisingly little difference in opinion.

In a significant break from conventional wisdom, the survey found that two out of three Christians believed that divorce was a reasonable solution to a problem marriage. In a seeming contradiction, the same survey found that a majority of Christians want the divorce process to be made more difficult. Yet another question determined that while Christians were twice as likely as non-Christians to prefer a "traditional" marriage, the Christian community was equally divided in support of traditional and more contemporary forms of marital relationships. Indeed, the rapid shift regarding the concept of marriage obligations held by Christians was exemplified by the fact that nearly half (45 percent) of the Christians interviewed stated that the children produced by unhappy marriage partners should not serve to keep the family intact. This figure represents a dramatic increase from the historic view of Christians, and was not greatly different from the percentage among non-Christians.[6]

These survey results indicate that attitudes about divorce and the family are in a state of radical transformation. Although Christians believe that marriage is intrinsically an important institution, they are buckling under the social and economic pressures that have challenged marital relationships and child-rearing obligations. Though once deemed a permanent bond between people, these days marriage is more commonly viewed as a union of convenience or expedience.

Abortion: The Tension of Personal Choice

The traditional Judeo-Christian ethic holds that human life is sacred, a gift from God that is to be protected. For centuries, abortion was commonly viewed as the practice of murder. The Bible spoke of the sanctity of life, and that perspective was thought to be reflected in our Constitution and the moral values upon which the nation was governed.

It took the turbulence of the sixties to instigate a relatively swift and dramatic revision in America's perceptions and laws on abortion. The "sexual revolution" was one of the more heralded aspects of the new lifestyle advocated by the Woodstock generation. Abortion was seen as a natural outgrowth of sexual freedom and the "do your own thing" philosophy that took root during the sixties. The credo of the new generation became, "do what you like, as long as it does not harm anyone else." Few people noticed how deftly that notion became ingrained in the mainstream of American thought. Today more than two-thirds of the adult public adhere to this philosophy.[7]

The influence of this individualistic mindset popularized during the sixties cannot be underestimated. One direct consequence of the "if it feels good, do it" outlook was the enormous increase in the number of unwanted pregnancies. This, in turn, resulted in the escalation of abortions (from 5,000 in 1966 to more than 100,000 in 1969).[8] This epidemic brought tremendous pressure against the system to legally sanction abortion-on-demand on the grounds that it was one of the personal freedoms implicitly guaranteed by the Constitution.

On January 22, 1973 the U.S. Supreme Court broke its silence on the abortion issue and ruled that the Constitution did indeed imply that abortion was a "right of personal privacy."

While much of the intensity of the debate has died in the wake of that decision, the behavioral effects have escalated dramatically.

- The number of abortions performed each year is now three times as great as it was in 1973. In 1983 alone, one and one-half million abortions were performed in America.

- Despite the continuing controversy over abortion on both medical and ethical grounds, the number of abortions conducted is increasing by nearly 10 percent annually.

- Since the Supreme Court's ruling in 1973, it is estimated that more than 10 million abortions have been performed.[9]

Much of the clamor against abortion-on-demand has come from the Christian community. Christians are more likely to see the moral implications of abortion than are non-Christians. Three out of four Christians (72 percent) described abortion as "morally wrong," compared to just 53 percent of the non-Christians. However, a large segment of the Christian population is unwilling to take a firm, public stand against abortion. Two out of five Christians contended that "there is no right or wrong side to abortion; it is a private matter to those involved."[10]

The fact that twenty million born-again Christians believe that abortion is a matter of private choice indicates again how Christians' views on the family are undergoing reformation.

Youth: The Tension of Maturation

Social analysts often refer to the nation's youth as its greatest natural resource. The process of maturation which young people experience is one of ubiquitous tension. Today more than ever, a myriad of role models compete for their attention and devotion. The choices made by our adolescents and young adults are significant in that these are the people who will inherit the country's wealth, manage the government, and continue to shape the nation's morals, values, and ethics. From the Christian perspective, today's teenagers are tomorrow's spiritual leaders. It behooves the Christian community to carefully foster viewpoints and behaviors that are consistent with those promoted in the Bible.

The Post-World War II Context

The close of the war brought home America's armed forces to celebrate their apparent success in "making the world safe for democracy." Fresh from its overseas victories and flexing its nuclear muscle, America believed that it was capable of guaranteeing unending liberty for itself and the rest of the "free world." Confident, perhaps to the point of arrogance, our young men returned to their land of opportunity to cash in on their potential—i.e., to pursue the material fruits of social freedom and economic prosperity.

As the parents of the 1950s dedicated themselves to the materialistic pursuit of happiness, the "baby-boom generation" was largely left to fend for itself. With the blessing of Dr. Spock, young minds were given new freedom to experiment, which led to new forms of communication in music and the media. Rock and roll emerged, with performers like Elvis Presley, Chuck Berry, and Buddy Holly offering young people a unique identity. Unlike previous generations, teenagers of the 1950s and early 1960s downplayed ethical foundations in establishing their values and standards. Rebellion loomed as one of the chief ingredients in the youth value structure.

Hollywood scrambled to capitalize on the evolving appetite of the young for tales of youth rebellion and ascension to power. Films like *Rebel Without a Cause* provided new heroes and a language that set youth apart from their elders. In a significant break with the past, young people no longer worried about explaining their philosophy of life; they simply lived it.

The rock and roll generation of the midsixties to early seventies impacted society in an unprecedented way, throwing out the old rules and replacing them with guidelines designed to satiate their immediate needs. Enormous shifts in the traditional values and attitudes of young people took place during this period in the areas of sexual morality, spirituality, family unions, patriotism, social status, and economic responsibility. Consider, for example, some of these shifts in opinions and beliefs held by American youth during that vital era of change:

- In 1969, 43 percent of college students said they would welcome wider acceptance of sexual freedom. By 1973, the figure had risen to more than 60 percent.

- The portion of college youth who felt religion was an important value in their life dropped from 38 percent to 28 percent during the same four-year period. Among noncollege youth, the same dynamic occurred, as the proportion slid from 65 percent to 42 percent.

- The sense of patriotism among college students declined from 35 percent to just 19 percent between 1969 and 1973. The same trend held true among noncollege youth, as the statistic plummeted to 40 percent from a high of 61 percent in 1969.

- Among noncollege youth, the importance of living a moral life was upheld by 78 percent in 1969, but by only 57 percent in 1973.[11]

The fervor of student radicalism and social revolution had largely died out by the midseventies, as American youth embraced a sense of egocentric pragmatism. The table on the following pages outlines the dramatic shifts in lifestyle common to eighteen- to twenty-two-year-olds that occurred within the span of a single decade.

What has happened since the onset of this new self-centered practicality?

National surveys conducted among high school students indicate that today's youth are continuing to move away from many of the beliefs and values espoused by their more radical predecessors. Trend data lead us to believe that the emerging generation of young people will enter the marketplace with a distinctly different view of life.

- More and more young people are adopting conservative political attitudes. While the proportion of high school students who describe themselves as liberals has dropped from 27 percent to 21 percent in five years, those who are self-identified conservatives has risen from 14 percent to 19 percent.

- The sense of hope and optimism that characterized the youth of the past has been replaced by a growing feeling of futility, loneliness, despair, and pessimism.

- A negative point of view regarding the character of other people dominates the thinking of today's young people. They have little faith in the trustworthiness, motives, and fairness of others.

- Fewer and fewer young adults maintain any interest in working for the common good. Over the past five years, interest has risen substantially in self-serving activities such as being successful in their occupation (from 52 percent to 57 percent); finding a job that offers a good chance for promotion (from 57 percent to 66 percent); obtaining a job that gives them the chance to earn a lot of money (up nine percentage points to 56 percent).

- Although young people have held a steady belief in the value of the family, most also believe that their parents could have done a far superior job in raising them.

- Religion remains a comparatively insignificant part of their lives. Less than one-third of the young view religion as being very important. Although two out of five attend worship services weekly, many of those students are coerced by parents into attending, and have little intention of remaining devoted churchgoers in the future.[12]

Table 2.2

**The Shift in Values and Behavior
Among College Students, from 1967-1975.**

Late 1960s	Mid-1970s
The campus rebellion is in full flower.	The campus rebellion is moribund.
New lifestyles and radical politics appear together: granny glasses, crunchy granola, commune living, pot smoking, and long hair seem inseparable from radical politics, sit-ins, student strikes, protest marches, draft card burnings.	An almost total divorce takes place between radical politics and new lifestyles.
A central theme on campus: the search for self-fulfillment in place of a conventional career.	A central theme on campus: how to find self-fulfillment within a conventional career.
Growing criticism of America as a "sick society."	Lessening criticism of America as a "sick society."
The women's movement has virtually no impact on youth values and attitudes.	Wide and deep penetration of women's liberation precepts is underway.
Violence on campus is condoned and romanticized; there are many acts of violence.	Violence-free campuses; the use of violence, even to achieve worthwhile objectives, is rejected.
The value of education is severely questioned.	The value of education is strongly endorsed.
A widening "generation gap" appears in values, morals, and	The young generation and older mainstream America move

Late 1960s	Mid-1970s
outlook, dividing young people (especially college youth) from their parents.	closer together in values, morals, and outlook.
A sharp split in social and moral values is found within the youth generation, between college students and the noncollege majority. The gap within the generation proves to be larger and more severe than the gap between the generations.	The gap within the generation narrows. Noncollege youth have virtually caught up with college students in adopting the new social and moral norms.
A new code of sexual morality, centering on greater acceptance of casual premarital sex, abortion, homosexuality, and extramarital relations is confined to a minority of college students.	The new sexual morality spreads both to mainstream college youth and also to mainstream working-class youth.
The challenge to the traditional work ethic is confined to the campus.	The work ethic appears strengthened on campus but is growing weaker among noncollege youth.
Harsh criticisms of major institutions, such as political parties, big business, the military, etc., are almost wholly confined to college students.	Criticism of some major institutions are tempered on campus but are taken up by working-class youth.
The universities and the military are major targets of criticism.	Criticism of the universities and the military decrease sharply.
The campus is the main locus of youthful discontent; noncollege youth is quiescent.	Campuses are quiescent, but many signs of latent discontent and dissatisfaction appear among working-class youth.
Much youthful energy and idealism is devoted to concern with minorities.	Concern for minorities lessens.
The political center of gravity of college youth: left/liberal.	No clear-cut political center of gravity: pressures in both directions, left and right.

Late 1960s	Mid-1970s
The New Left is a force on campus: there are growing numbers of radical students.	The New Left is a negligible factor on campus: the number of radical students declines sharply.
Concepts of law and order are anathema to college students.	College students show greater acceptance of law-and-order requirements.
The student mood is angry, embittered, and bewildered by public hostility.	There are a few signs of anger or bitterness and little overt concern with public attitudes toward students.

While this information could hardly be described as good news for the future, there is some cause for hope. If the student leaders are studied as a separate entity, a vastly different picture emerges of what the future may have in store.

Like all young people, the high school elite—those who receive the highest grades, are most active in extra-curricular activities, and are most likely to continue their education after high school—are turning more conservative in their outlook. This transition is evident in personal matters as well as on social issues. Examples of the dramatic change in views include:

- Support for legalized abortion has declined from 60 percent to 46 percent.

- The ratio of the student elite who approve of premarital sex has been reduced by one-third, from 54 percent to 38 percent.

- A growing proportion of student leaders would prefer to marry a virgin (up from 49 percent to 62 percent).

- Sexual activity was decreased; only one in five student leaders admits to having experienced sexual intercourse, a drop of 25 percent since 1972.[13]

Perhaps the most encouraging news for Christians concerns the spiritual perspective of the high school elite. Three out of four claim that religion plays an important part in their life today; almost nine out of ten consider themselves to be part of an organized religious group; and two out of three say that the religious faith to which they ascribe is a matter of their own choice, not of their parents. This latter fact is particularly significant, since it represents twice as many students who have personally investigated spiritual matters as a decade ago.[14]

The Road to Survival

Divorce, abortion, and the rebellion of our youth are only three of the tensions mounting against the vitality of the family unit. A host of other equally serious pressures are grating against it. Homosexuality, infanticide, euthanasia, and the feminist movement are all examples of the types of forces that are constantly challenging the survival of the conventional family.

The reaction of the Christian community to the attack against the family—indifference or a willingness to surrender Christian principles in many cases—bodes poorly for the future of the family as we know it today. The attitudes and values of all Americans—Christians as well as non-Christians—are steadily being shifted away from those espoused by the Bible. Gradually the debate is changing from one of secular versus Christian values to one stream of secular thought against a variation of the secular humanist philosophy.

Both the leadership and the laity within the Christian community must shoulder the blame for this calamity. The leadership of the Christian community has to a large extent failed to provide effective biblical guidance. Pastors and evangelists have proven themselves to be inadequate role models, necessitating a "do as I say, not as I do" posture in many cases. Teaching has been sporadic and short-sighted on issues related to the family. Some teaching has been downright misguided (as James Dobson has shown, for example, regarding the frequent admonitions given to the "submissive wife").

The Christian mass has fallen prey to such weak shepherding partially because of its own naivete. Research has indicated that millions of Christians fail to comprehend the connection between God's teaching through the Bible, the secular humanist philosophy that is so prevalent in our current age, and their own daily activities. Events have consequences. Too many Christians, however, do not see the "big picture" in life, and ignore Paul's warning that we are constantly engaged in spiritual warfare. This ineptness is a result of the biblical illiteracy of Christians and their inability to apply scriptural principles to their daily lives. Spiritual values are commonly thought to be operative only on Sundays, leaving the average Christian unarmed in his daily struggles in the marketplace.

While the crisis of survival confronting the family looms larger than life on the one hand, there are avenues open to us to address the crisis with confidence and hope. Indeed, if the best defense is a good offense, Christians must seek to develop a sense of Christian philosophy as it relates to the family and to promote that perspective as convincingly as the secular humanist champions his vacuous philosophy.

How do we start? The initial step must be turning to the Scripture to identify what God has told us about the family. The Bible is our key tangible resource in discovering God's will for the family. Christians need to recall, if not learn anew, that the family is one of God's chosen instruments for promoting his Kingdom as well as providing us with fellowship, personal fulfillment, and inner strength. Every Christian needs to become intimately acquainted with Paul's description of love, found in 1 Corinthians 13.

> This love of which I speak is
>> slow to lose patience—it looks for a way to be constructive; it is not possessive: it is neither anxious to impress nor does it cherish inflated ideas of its own importance. Love has good manners and does not pursue selfish advantage. It is not touchy. It does not keep account of evil or gloat over the wickedness of other people.
> On the contrary,
>> it shares the joy of those who live by the truth. Love knows no limit to its endurance, no end to its trust, no fading of its hope; it can outlast anything. Love never fails. (vv. 4-8, *Phillips*)

If Christian people were to study and memorize and apply these principles, how could they justify the dissolution of their marriages? Through similar study and reflection on Jesus' words about adultery and divorce in Matthew 5:27-32, how could Christian adults defend their immorality and quest for personal fulfillment at the expense of their families? If Christian people were to take seriously the teaching in Ephesians 5:21—6:4 regarding gentle submission to one another for the sake of Jesus, following his example for us, there undoubtedly would be much less household strife and conflict. Christians need to show the world how they are different, and that difference must be the way they live the love that Christ commands us to implement in our daily behavior. Along with serious Bible study we must be diligent in prayer, seek God's will, and reiterate our trust in his power and guidance.

Once familiar with the Scriptures, Christians must take the bold stands that the Bible exhorts, fully cognizant that the principles we support will often clash with those preferred by the world system. This may require a significant reshaping of our personal priorities in life to conform with the best interests of the family. Again, the Bible leads us to the understanding that earthly treasures and pleasures are transitory at best; but standing up for the values taught by Jesus will increase our reward in Heaven (Luke 12:13-21).

Christians need not approach familial pressures or debate as lone rangers. If we are unable to rely upon family members for guidance, then seeking the counsel of godly people, whether professional Christian counselors, church leaders, or merely good Christian friends, is a scriptural means of addressing problems that confront us. To their credit, evangelical seminaries have undertaken a broad-based effort to upgrade the quality and breadth of their counseling programs for the clergy. There is little excuse today for those Christians who snap under the pressure of marital or other family-related problems simply because they refused to share their burden with someone else. Part of the purpose of belonging to a body of believers is so that sharing can occur, during the good times and the bad.

Survey data clearly indicate that Christians have largely withdrawn from the debate on matters such as abortion and child-rearing practices because of an inferiority complex. Literally millions of born-again believers feel some need to apologize to the world for their beliefs and for their attempts to apply their beliefs to the way they deal with family matters. Christians need to turn that thinking around. They should seek an apology from those who have tried so ardently to remove Christian principles from the realm of debate and acceptable behavior. Christianity is not merely a set of religious values, but a way of life. While Jesus never claimed that the path would be an easy one, he did claim that his way provides all the solutions necessary to live a successful and fulfilling life. Rather than meekly trying to implement our principles without causing a stir around us, we are charged to teach others by our example and our words. As Jesus instructed, "Let your light shine before men, that they may see your good works and give glory to your Father who is in heaven" (Matt. 5:16).

Some writers have called the present struggle the

"battle for the family." That is an understatement. A veritable war is being waged. Christians may well represent the last hope for the survival of the family, one of God's chief means of working on earth. But unless the Christian body awakens to the scope and significance of this war, the casualties will be great.

3 Divided We Stand, United We Fall: Educating the Next Generation of Christians

From Alexis de Tocqueville to John Kennedy, many observers of world affairs have argued that the critical characteristic that sets America apart from the rest of the world is her commitment to education of the masses. In practical terms, education is important not merely as a means of transferring information from one generation to the next, but also as a means of socializing the young—that is, imparting to our youth the fundamental values and attitudes that distinguish American culture.

For those who measure interest and commitment in terms of dollars and cents, consider that in 1984 alone, more than $100 billion will be spent on education in the United States. Next to national defense, more government funds are devoted to public education than to any other budget item. By spending 7 percent of the nation's gross national product on education—double what was spent in 1950—the United States has solidified its standing as the most prolific supporter of education in the world.

Yet, in spite of the unchallenged importance assigned to public education, the billions of dollars spent on educational activities, and the hundreds of thousands of man-hours devoted to the teaching and administering of educational programs, Americans feel cheated. Over the past decade, public opinion polls have consistently identified public disenchantment with the public school system. Parents throughout the land gripe that the system provides a mediocre education. Americans have held fast to the belief that a decent education for all people is both desirable and possible, but they openly question whether they are getting their money's worth. As this chapter will show, a movement within the Christian community is afoot to redefine the objectives and responsibilities of education in America.

Shifting the Responsibility
In colonial times, the family was the primary source of education. Youngsters were introduced to language, social customs, modes of behavior, vocational skills, and value systems by their parents. For many decades parents tacitly assumed that one of their familial duties was to prepare their offspring to cope with society. As the nation grew and the economy changed, the household character was altered; small schools operated by the churches emerged as an alternative to home education. As in the home setting, the curriculum at church-operated schools often included a heavy emphasis on the Bible as a source of spiritual growth and moral concepts. It was even used as a basic text for introducing reading and writing skills.

It was not until the mid-1800s that "public education"—that is, a standardized, comparatively homogeneous education, in which the government assumed a major role—began to emerge as yet another educational option. This approach to education, which Americans take for granted today, was a novel concept. Indeed, the authors of the Constitution made no provisions in that document for government involvement in what was considered an exclusive family responsibility. Even the courts of that day argued forcefully that it was not only the parents' right to take full responsibility for educating their children, but court opinions "elevated parental rights in this area above any possible interest of the state; the parents' right to educate their own children was equated with a democratic freedom."[1]

Nevertheless, as America entered a period of tremendous growth in technology and ideas in the mid-1800s, public education emerged as one of the country's most profound social transformations. The American concept of public education was both unique and, by the standards established in the 1840s and 1850s, successful. The American education system soon became a model for countries around the world who aspired to universal literacy and who believed that the explosive growth of America was attributable to its emphasis on educating the public.

Quality Drops, Discontent Rises
Barely a century after the introduction of public education in America, the decaying roots of that system were exposed as never before. The nation's educational leaders were challenged by the publication of scathing re-

views of the education system, such as *Crisis in the Classroom*. In that exposé, author Charles Silberman cited evidence of the decline of standards and performance in public education, and called for sweeping modifications in the leadership, curricula, and instructional methods that characterized our public school network.[2]

Supporting Silberman's argument were the trends evident in various test scores of public school students. One of the most popular tests used throughout the nation is the Scholastic Aptitude Test (SAT), administered to high school seniors who wish to attend college. Although the test is not a measure of intelligence, it is used as a standard measure of students' abilities to solve mathematical and language problems. As the accompanying graphs illustrate, test-score averages have been dropping steadily since 1967. The deterioration of skill has been especially noticeable in the area of language ("verbal") capabilities.[3]

National attitudinal surveys have uncovered a parallel between public and expert opinion regarding the performance of our public schools. Since 1974, studies conducted by the Gallup Organization have identified a dramatic decrease in people's satisfaction with public schools. In 1974, 48 percent of the adults in this country felt that the public schools in their communities were doing an "above average" job of educating students. By 1983, that figure had dropped to just 31 percent. In fact, only one-third as many people as ten years earlier felt that the schools were doing "A" quality work (down from 18 percent in 1974 to 6 percent in 1983).[4]

The Gallup data also provide some insight into what is troubling Americans about their public schools. Since 1974, the most commonly voiced complaint about the schools has been the lack of discipline exerted within the classroom. Nearly one out of every three adults identified disciplinary problems as their major concern. The widespread use of drugs at public schools, poor curriculum, and slipping academic standards have also ranked near the top of the list of concerns each year during the past decade.

Beyond the disturbing nature of these problems, the related statistics are alarming because of their consistency. Parents are saying that public education is neither as good as it used to be, nor making any discernible strides toward improvement. Perhaps as evidence of a snowballing deterioration of confidence in the schools, increasing numbers of parents are indicating that the quality of teachers has also tailed off in recent years.[5]

Public schools located in major cities are the worst-off. Urban parents are twice as likely as nonurban parents to feel that their local schools are doing an inadequate job.[6]

Of tremendous significance is the fact that more parents identify behavioral problems than academic concerns as the most serious deficiency of the public institutions. The implication may relate more to the capabilities of parents than to the performance of the schools. Unable to discipline their own children, many parents expect the public schools to provide behavioral training in addition to more traditional intellectual guidance. Many of these parents have lost faith in the public schools because of a perceived failure in the institutions' disciplinary performance. Too few of these parents pause to reflect on the validity of their expectation that schools provide basic behavior modeling and training.

Christian Schools as an Alternative

Research reveals that Christian parents are not taking the failure of the public schools lightly. An alternative that is gaining momentum—literally by the day—is the Christian school.[7] How significant is the exodus from public schools to these Bible-centered institutions? Consider the following:

- Although precise figures do not exist, there are an estimated 10,000 Christian schools currently in operation. That represents more than double the number of Christian schools that existed just five years ago. In fact, the universe of Christian schools is expanding at the rate of nearly three new schools each day.[8]

- In 1950, 91 percent of all school-aged children attended public schools. Today, only 74 percent attend public schools.[9]

- Based on available figures, it appears that the number of students enrolled in Christian schools has jumped from 731,000 students in 1978 to about 1,530,000 students in 1983. That is an increase of 110 percent in just five years.[10]

This transition is all the more meaningful when the financial implications are considered. Parents who withdraw their children from public schools pay a stiff penalty for that action. Tax dollars dedicated to public education are estimated to cost the average household $2100 per year. In addition to paying that tax levy, the family sending its child to a Christian school pays an average of $600 per year more for tuition, books, and other related expenses—about 30 percent above the tax charge.[11] The more children a family has enrolled in Christian schools, the more severe the financial burden becomes.

Parents who remove their children from the public schools believe the benefits of Christian schools sufficiently offset the costs. A mother with two youngsters attending Christian schools summed up the feelings of many by stating:

> These are the years when children take on their character. I want my kids to grow up in a Christian environment while still getting a solid education. At the local (public) schools, all they came home with was foul language and stories about fights. They rarely had any homework. I don't know how these kids were supposed to learn anything there.

Some parents, while enticed by the potential of Christian schools, are concerned that if their children attend Christian schools they will be at a competitive disadvantage when applying for college admission. This is a sensitive area to many Christian educators, who claim that their teaching methods and their graduates are superior to those of the public schools, but have few facts to support those claims.

One professional organization, the Association of

Christian Schools International (ACSI), has taken the initial step toward substantiating the claim that Christian schools provide a better learning environment. In a study conducted in 1983, students enrolled in ACSI schools scored significantly higher on a standardized achievement test than students at non-Christian schools. This finding was constant for all grade levels—first through twelfth. At a minimum, the ACSI students were five months above the national average in educational achievement, and they were as much as sixteen months above the national average at the eleventh grade level.[12]

What does the future portend? While it is unrealistic to support the claim of one study that Christian schools will encompass 52 percent of all students by the year 1990, continued rapid growth will occur. By the end of this decade, as many as three million students will likely be enrolled in Christian schools.

The Fastest-Growing Alternative: Home Education

America is entering an era in which a substantial number of Christian parents are unwilling to entrust the education of their children to any formal institution, be it public, private, or even Christian. In the sixties and seventies, the response of such people might have been to enroll their children in "alternative" schools. In the 1980s, the increasingly prevalent response is going to be education conducted within the home.

Home education has endured in America despite odds heavily stacked against its survival. A number of respected, national leaders in this century were the products of home education. The list includes Franklin Roosevelt and Woodrow Wilson, George Patton and Douglas MacArthur, and Pearl Buck.[13]

According to Dr. Raymond Moore, a leader in the home education movement and director of Hewitt Research Foundation, the most common motive for choosing home education is to protect children from the anti-Christian, human-deifying influences that permeate the public schools. According to Moore, "at least 85-90 percent of today's home schoolers are motivated by religious convictions. These parents do not want their children taught within a humanist environment."

Home education is perceived as such a radical response to the situation that legislators and journalists have turned it into a bona fide public issue. The judicial system has entered the fray as well, defining home education as a challenge to statutes concerning recognized religious and personal freedoms. One state, Mississippi, has legislatively condoned home education, and there are several other states that may well follow suit shortly. In the meantime, however, hundreds of families are facing legal battles over their decision to educate their own children—and are spending a fortune to defend their right to do so.[14]

The various pressures bearing down on these families have not arrested the growth of home education. It is currently estimated that between 500,000 and 1,000,000 children are receiving in-home instruction. Thanks to the media's recent interest in the issue, nearly half of the adult public who have school-aged children are aware of the home education movement.[15]

The explosion in the number and range of independent support functions provides further evidence that the movement is for real: home educator associations, newsletters for involved parents, books about the movement, legal counsel available to assist parents challenged by government authorities, and a variety of curricula designed specifically for in-home instruction.

In addition to those parents who are totally committed to home education for their children, there are others who support the movement, but not as robustly. Some in-home educators, for example, harbor anxieties over the "separation effects" caused by keeping their children out of the mainstream. These parents have adopted a compromise solution. They will teach their children at home during their initial school years and eventually enroll them in a formal school. They believe that by providing a Christian world view and value system during their child's formative years, the child will be better equipped to navigate through the dangers of the humanist philosophy they sense in the public schools.

The impact of the home education movement transcends the number of students currently going through their academic paces at home. The movement has, in part, helped to raise the national consciousness regarding educational quality. Just as importantly (from a Christian viewpoint), many parents are for the first time reflecting on their role in the education of their children. They are realizing the public schools are an option, not a monopoly. Indeed, while the thought of tangling with the judicial and legislative power structures overwhelms some, uncounted thousands of parents are taking more responsibility for their children's learning by supplementing the teaching of the public schools. Shunning a direct confrontation over the right to control the educational process, these parents have chosen to instruct their children in areas neglected by the schools, and to balance the humanist perspective of the public schools with a Christian perspective.

John Naisbitt argues that the home education movement will draw its strength from a developing social trend away from institutional reliance, in favor of self-reliance.[16] That explanation presents a naive dismissal of the spiritual motivations underlying the home education drive. The staunch religious commitment that serves as the foundation for most decisions to go the home education route intimates that America is witnessing the initial stage of a fundamental rejection of widely accepted cultural values and norms. While there is insufficient evidence to claim that a religious-based, educational revolution of major proportions is in the making, it is true that the secular-humanist orientation of the present educational system, and the socio-cultural changes it has helped to bring about, have challenged the essential truths by which Christians live. Consequently, many Christians have adopted home education as an initial stab at meeting the challenge. Far from being a transitory fad, or a superficial reaction to a perceived threat, the movement represents both the thoughtful dismissal of accepted socialization practices, and a significant step toward addressing the very justification of secularized, institutional education. Expect to see the number of students being educated at home to more than double by the end of this decade.

The Threat to Christian Colleges

The educational revolution will not stop at the elementary and secondary school levels. On the college front, changes are occurring in the type of education desired by students, the facilities required to provide a modern education, and the costs associated with earning a college degree. Many of these changes in the character of higher education bode poorly for the Christian colleges of the nation. The problems facing colleges—Christian or secular—are generally the same. The difference lies in the capacity of these different types of institutions to cope with societal change.

Consider these realities confronting Christian colleges:

- *The pool of potential and enrolling students is shrinking.* Between 1980 and 1990, the total number of Christian high school graduates will plummet by 20 percent, from 550,000 students in 1980 to 450,000 a decade later. This is due mostly to the national "age pyramid," in which the "baby boomers" (children conceived in the midfifties and early sixties) have matured, and the postbaby boom fertility rate declined substantially. The anticipated pattern of decline has already set in. Christian colleges are experiencing decreases in the number of applicants, the percentage of applicants who qualify for admission (either academically or financially), and the percentage of applicants who enroll. For instance, among schools affiliated with the Christian College Coalition, the size of the full-time freshman class in 1982 contracted by 7.3 percent in comparison to the 1981 figures; and the graduate student populations at those institutions dropped 2.6 percent in one year (contrasted to a 4.3 percent increase at secular schools). Consider that 11 percent of the Coalition colleges withstood at least a 20 percent loss of enrollment in the one-year span.[17]

- *Tuition costs are becoming prohibitive.* Lacking government subsidies, Christian colleges rely more heavily than most schools upon tuition fees as their revenue base. The spiraling cost of operations—salaries, facilities, maintenance, advertising and marketing, and so forth—will require that the average cost of tuition over four years leap from $24,000 today to $60,000 for students entering college in 1992. As further evidence of the fiscal problems of Christian colleges, note that the financial aid cutbacks wrought by the Reagan Administration have subtracted nearly $100 million per year of aid that would have helped Christian college students meet their tuition obligations. As a consequence, many students who were dependent on those loans, grants, and other forms of aid have been forced to attend less expensive state and community colleges.[18]

- *Christian colleges have largely resisted the move to make college a "vocational training ground."* Christian college leaders are struggling with the core of their educational philosophy: whether they should continue to provide an education that produces "generalists," or whether they should join the new wave of educators who have acquiesced to parental desires and financial pressures by offering an academically-oriented occupational training program. Times have changed. In 1965, 21 percent of all college students pursued a liberal arts major; today, only 7 percent do so. In 1968, about 25 percent of the college population sought degrees in business or engineering; today, almost twice as many collegians are enrolled in those "practical" courses of study. Yet, Christian schools have largely resisted the mass movement and retained their liberal arts identity.[19]

• *The competition for college students is becoming increasingly fierce.* Secular colleges and universities are undergoing many of the same "shrinking pains" that threaten Christian colleges. Through the application of more advanced marketing and advertising techniques, recruiting and image-building campaigns have mitigated some of the difficulties for many schools. One of the strengths that many secular schools emphasize is their reputation for providing a high-quality education. By many of the standard measures, Christian colleges cannot make such claims. One survey among the nation's university and college presidents found that among the 1308 four-year institutions in America, 110 stood out as being particularly good. Among those 110 schools, only 18—which is 16 percent of the aggregate—were Christian colleges. While some would argue that this represents an outstanding showing by Christian colleges—since they represented a minority of the total schools eligible for consideration in the survey—others point out that being outnumbered 92-18, in absolute terms, puts Christian colleges at a relative disadvantage in the highly combative sweepstakes for new students.[20]

Based on these figures and trends, it is likely that the coming decade will see a significant shift in the character of the Christian college system. Financial pressures will cause in the neighborhood of 10 to 15 percent to close their doors for good. Many of the remaining schools will survive by reducing staff and cutting back in areas that are already lean.

To their credit, Christian colleges generally have adjusted to the computer age. Even among the few Christian colleges that have not yet installed computers for their students, the major deterrent is not so much philosophical as financial: the hardware and software costs are simply out of range when pennies are being pinched to make ends meet.

At this early stage in the age of computers, merely possessing a limited quantity of the machines should temporarily suffice, at least for the purposes of impressing potential recruits that the school is modern. However, Christian colleges are already lagging behind their secular counterparts when it comes to the availability of on-campus computer facilities.

A special survey of American colleges showed that it is the small Christian college that is least adequately equipped with computer hardware. Among Christian colleges with seven hundred or fewer students, there was an average of one terminal in place for every fifty-six students. At larger Christian colleges, the ratio improved to one terminal per forty-six students. These averages paled in comparison to the ratio that characterized a sampling of the prime secular institutions (one terminal per thirty students). As the significance of computers expands in the marketplace, this disadvantage may cause some Christian institutions to lose whatever competitive edge they had over schools with superior computer facilities.[21]

Looking Ahead

Christians are making their presence felt in educational circles. In making waves, though, Christians who are involved in the alternatives to the public schools must be prepared to answer some tough questions that will be posed by friend and foe alike. The adequacy with which Christians—parents, students, Christian schools, and Christian colleges—address those inquiries will in large part determine how society will react.

Christian Parents

The largest burden of all falls on the shoulders of Christian parents. In the wake of the fuss they are stirring over the mediocrity of public schools, intense public scrutiny will be focused on these parents. They must anticipate the nature of the evaluation they will experience and prepare accordingly.

To start with, Christian parents must accept the responsibility to discipline their own children. Abdicating that function to the public schools has resulted in blanket chaos. But more to the point, all Christians have a scriptural obligation to teach their children how to behave. Leaving the tough aspects of child-raising, such as discipline, to the schools is improper.

The home school movement ought to motivate and encourage all Christian parents to become intimately involved in their children's education. Regardless of the educational experiences of parents and their children, parents have a biblical obligation to nurture and protect their offspring. Only through firsthand participation in the education process can parents know what their children are being exposed to. If the educational experiences that occur outside the home are predominantly good, parents can build upon that foundation during family time. If those experiences are not good, remedial action should be taken immediately. God entrusts parents with an awesome responsibility in the rearing of children. The magnitude of that responsibility is not an acceptable excuse for a job haphazardly done; indeed, the greater the task, the more care must be taken.

In making decisions about the type of education preferred for children, some parents become so wrapped up in the philosophical trappings of the decision that they neglect the most important element of the equation: what would really be best for their child? This is not to assert that these parents intend harm to their children. Quite to the contrary, they get involved in making such decisions only because they want the best for their young ones. However, too many parents forget about the unique characteristics and qualities of each child, and treat him or her like a mass-produced object. Christian schools are not right for all students, whether they need Christian training and nourishment or not. There are numerous cases of Christian students who were miserable in a Christian school and flourished once transferred to a public institution. Parents must be sensitive to the unique nature of each of their children, who need to be dealt with as individuals with identifiable, specific needs. The parent is obliged to make every effort to nurture that child in the fullest, most effective manner, whether that requires public schooling, a Christian school, or in-home training.

More broadly, Christian adults must assume the role of overseer to the public schools. "Taking over" is not the issue; providing constructive input is. In many cases, public schools are not performing up to standards because parents are not holding the schools accountable. Just as problematic, some parents hold the schools "secretly accountable"; they rate the schools according to specific standards, but never describe those standards to the schools. When tensions climax in the withdrawal of their children from the school, the public school personnel are often shocked, then embittered; nothing has been gained from the experience. Christian parents should be willing to attempt to correct wrongs that exist in the public schools.

In fact, Christian parents appear to have given relatively limited consideration to the side effects of creating a separatist Christian culture. When Jesus said we are to be the "salt of the earth," he was commanding believers to work on his behalf in the midst of a corrupt society, not from the outside looking in. There are situations where Christians need to insulate themselves from society. However, such separation must be conscious and warranted. In the case of separate Christian schools and educational systems, Christians need to carefully assess the implications of isolating themselves from the very people to whom they are called to minister. Believers cannot hope to influence the world for Christ if they refuse to interact with that world. Separate Christian educational systems make all the sense in the world—sometimes, for some people. This is a very personal, conscious decision with which each family should earnestly wrestle.

Christian Schools

Christian schools are the "new kid on the block." As such, the existing power structure (public schools, legislators, journalists, parents) will be watching every move they make. That is not bad; in fact, it gives the Christian schools a tremendous opportunity to really show their detractors and doubters what good education is all about.

However, this means that the Christian schools must be totally committed to quality. Curriculum must be relevant and first-rate. Teachers must be superb communicators, knowledgeable, and caring. Facilities must meet reasonable standards. There must be a noticeable difference between what the public schools have to offer and what the Christian schools provide. Because the Christian schools are the alternative, they cannot merely be "as good" as the public institutions— they must be better. A number of Christian schools which were studied as part of the research for this book fell short of this imperative because they had a different goal: survival. To serve their highest purpose, though, Christian schools should strive to reach the highest plateau of performance. Young Christians deserve no less.

Christian Colleges

Christian colleges play a major role in the ability of the Christian elementary and secondary schools to provide the best in education. Very simply, they must provide a sufficient quantity of highly qualified Christian teachers to fill available positions. In the past, the colleges have done a commendable job of producing such educators. However, as college enrollments drop and the need for Christian teachers increases, Christian colleges must gear up to keep supply on par with demand.

4 Technology Takes Over: The Media in America

Next to sleeping and working for a living, Americans devote more time to the media than to any other daily activity. In a typical day, the average American spends eight hours on the job, seven hours sleeping, and nearly five hours absorbing messages from the media. What little time is left over is divided among the other priorities in people's lives, such as eating, exercising, and nurturing the family.

Not long ago almost all media activities were described as "leisure options" and "work alternatives." Today the media have become an integral part of people's daily routine. Television viewing, in particular, has become a staple in the American way of life. In the average household "the tube" is aglow seven hours during the day, and the typical adult views more than three hours of programming each day. Three out of four adults listen to the radio on a daily basis. Four out of five adults read newspapers every day. Even the less prolific media—magazines, books, movies—involve millions of people each day. America has, in the space of just fifty years, become a media-mad society, a land of multimedia addicts.

While our media obsession makes for interesting conversation and reflections, studies have proven that our expanding media diet has some serious behavioral implications. For instance, social analysts widely agree that the media are a major agent of change and assimilation in American society. The media transmit more than information and entertainment; they have a tremendous impact on our values, attitudes, behavior, and perceptions of the world.[1] Prior to the media proliferation, Americans relied heavily upon their personal experiences for insight into the world and humanity. These days, many form their opinions about the world from what the media impart to them as reality.

A new twist has been added to the study of the effect of the media. In prior decades analysts concentrated on understanding the influence of the content transmitted (i.e., the message). Today the challenge has been expanded due to the recent introduction of new media and radically new applications of existing media. Computer and satellite technology have greatly transformed the communications environment. New media such as direct satellite broadcasting have been born. New applications of existing media—for example, videotex and cable television—have further altered the media landscape.

Impetuous and Unpredictable: Television Reaches Midlife Crisis

Television is now in its fourth decade. The changes in the medium that have occurred in the eighties, however, are perhaps the most profound yet. Methods of broadcast delivery as well as program content have undergone unparalleled change.

One aspect has remained constant: Americans are firmly committed to television. The time people spend watching televised programs has steadily increased over the past twenty years. In the last four years alone the average time spent watching TV has jumped from 2.9 hours to 3.3 hours daily—a 14 percent rise.[2] As further evidence of our nation's passion for television, note that not only are 98 percent of the homes in this country equipped with a television set, but the average home contains two sets, and three out of four homes have at least one color set.[3]

Christians, as a group, are somewhat less committed to television than non-Christians. While the typical Christian adult will spend just under three hours a day viewing TV, the average non-Christian will spend an extra half hour per day watching programs. The significance of this difference becomes clear only when placed within the context of what is being absorbed during those hours each day.

Television programs—especially those shown by the networks—have incited constant criticism. Program research has provided substance to many of the criticisms, finding that instances of violence, sex, and verbal profanity occur with alarming consistency throughout network programming. Worse, these offenses are occurring with greater frequency than ever before.

Psychologists have carefully studied the effects of violence shown on television. Despite heated debate regarding the absolute level of influence on behavior exerted by the viewing of violence on TV, the consensus is that there is a significant relationship between watching violence and behaving violently. Such conclusions have been arrived at by government and academic sources alike. A few of the more disturbing findings regarding violence on television could be summarized as follows:

- Upon graduation from high school, the average person has already witnessed more than 13,000 violent deaths on television. Note that this figure includes only deaths; thousands of additional other violent behaviors are concurrently viewed by these young and impressionable individuals.[4]

- Parents, traditionally regarded as the chief agents of socialization for their children, appear to be losing their influence. Increasingly, parents are losing their ability to counteract the negative behaviors and aggressions learned by their children as a result of watching acts of violence on television.[5]

- As a distinct category of programming, the shows that are broadcast on weekend mornings and early afternoons are the most violent of all. Between 1967-1978, there were 7.5 violent acts per hour during prime time programming. During those same years, weekend daytime children's programs portrayed eighteen violent acts per hour. One researcher concluded that the continued exposure of youngsters to violence made them increasingly insensitive to such behavior.[6]

- In addition to the concerns listed above, research reports issued by the National Institute of Mental Health, the U.S. Surgeon General, and the National

PTA describe various other negative behavioral effects produced by exposure to television violence. Some of the more serious potential results include the development of a distorted perception of reality; psychological paranoia; diminished expectations regarding the quality of life; and disruption of social roles and responsibilities borne by parents, educators, broadcasters, advertisers, and government representatives.[7]

Network executives have offered a twofold response to criticisms about the negative effects of televised violence. Not surprisingly, the networks have tried to refute the validity of the studies that have condemned television violence. More importantly, the controversy seems to have increased their insistence on promoting violence through programming.

The Fall 1983 television season proved to be one of the most violent in the history of broadcasting. As the data in Table 4.1 show, the number of times in which programs showed violent incidents increased by 68 percent over 1981. The average hour of prime time programming in late 1983 contained nearly ten cases of violence. The prime purveyors of violence were NBC and ABC.

The data also show that sex and profanity are becoming increasingly prevalent in network shows. Between 1981 and 1983, the number of times in which viewers were exposed to profane language increased 40 percent; the frequency of sexual activity (both suggested and exhibited) also increased 40 percent. Even many who support the inclusion of sexual content on television are shocked to learn that four out of five scenes which suggest sexual intercourse involve persons who are not married!

Public opinion studies have suggested that the viewing public is concerned about the content of the programs being broadcast. How, then, can the acceleration of offensive content be explained?

One potential explanation relates to the general apathy of the viewing public. Despite concerns about watching too much violence, sex, and profanity, the audience has been unwilling to take any significant action against the sponsors of such programming. For instance, although 35 percent of the public said that they favored the idea of boycotting products advertised by the sponsors of violent programs, only 2 percent had actually taken such action.[8] Although televised violence was felt to be a major concern among adults, only three out of ten parents supported the idea of removing violent programs from the air altogether. Fewer than one in three parents said that they restricted the viewing hours and habits of their children. Thus, despite expressions of dissatisfaction with the nature of current programs, people have not backed their concern with meaningful action.[9]

Many individuals—including millions of born-again Christians—believe that as the networks face stiffer competition for viewers from other entertainment sources, such as cable television and the movies, the quality of programming will improve. A recent study of the major television executives and creative leaders of the TV industry, however, suggests that such optimism is ill-conceived. Far from reflecting the background and interests of the public that they serve, those who direct the path of television programming have a different agenda than that of the Christian viewing public.

Table 4.1

**Trends in Sex, Violence, and Profanity
in Network Prime-time Television Programming (1981-1983)**

	Total instances of sex	Total instances of violence	Total instances of profanity
Fall 1981	1939	1557	1557
Fall 1982	2019	2149	915
Fall 1983	2717	2149	2188
1981-83 change	+40%	+68%	+40%
NBC-1983	1048	973	663
ABC-1983	884	917	509
CBS-1983	785	720	1028

	Sex outside of marriage— instances of suggested intercourse	Sex inside of marriage— instances of suggested intercourse	Percent of instances of suggested intercourse occurring between unmarried people
Fall 1981	337	76	82%
Fall 1982	302	85	78%
Fall 1983	405	74	85%
1981-83 change	+20%	−3%	—
NBC-1983	150	20	88%
ABC-1983	126	26	83%
CBS-1983	129	28	82%

Sources: *Spring 1982 Television Monitoring Program,* Coalition for Better Television.
Fall 1982 Television Monitoring Program, Coalition for Better Television.
Fall 1983 Television Monitoring Program, Coalition for Better Television.

Television executives—a relatively tiny group of individuals who are responsible for producing, writing, and managing the programs watched in America's eighty-three million television households each week— are truly an elite corps in American society (see Table

4.2). Almost exclusively made up of white males, the television elite are highly educated (they are three times as likely as the average viewer to have a college degree); extremely wealthy (one out of four make more than $500,000 annually); and are generally liberal in their political views. From a religious perspective, the TV elite have relatively little in common with the American public, much less with the Christian population. Only one out of every fourteen television executives attends church regularly, and a majority have either a Jewish background or no religious affiliation at all.

Table 4.2

Background Characteristics of Television Executives and Leaders, Compared to the Television Viewing Public

Characteristic	Television Executives	Television Viewers
Male	98%	48%
White	99	87
Raised Jewish	59	2
College graduate	75	24
Earn $75,000 or more per year	96	4
Politically liberal	75	14
Attend church regularly	7	55
No religious affiliation	44	10

Sources: Linda Lichter, S. Robert Lichter, Stanley Rothman, "Hollywood and America: The Odd Couple," *Public Opinion*, January 1983, pp. 54-58.

Lifestyle Trends in America, survey by American Resource Bureau, Wheaton, IL, 1983.

The liberal perspective and lack of religious involvement may help explain the secular humanist approach to morality by television leaders. Almost unani-

mously (97 percent), the executives indicated that women have the right to decide on having an abortion. Four out of five executives (80 percent) stated that homosexuality was not wrong. Amazingly, a majority (51 percent) declared that adultery was not wrong.[10]

Perhaps the most chilling realization of all concerns the notion harbored by most of these men as to their ultimate objectives for television. Two out of three TV executives suggested that television should promote social reform. This, in itself, is not necessarily shocking. Many people would agree that American society could stand social reform in certain respects. Indeed, many executives at Christian television stations view their mission—broadcasting to bring about spiritual revival—to be a type of social reform.

It is the nature of the reform sought by the secular TV elite that warrants widespread Christian concern. These men overwhelmingly reject the notion that current programming is too critical of traditional values. Further, they argue that television does not offer too much sexually oriented content. (Surprisingly, they did admit that there was too much violence in programs.)[11]

The ruling elite of television, then, sees itself neither as operating a medium striving to provide harmless entertainment, nor to reflect the social and political values of its audience. The select few who have control of the medium are consciously striving to transform American society, through television, to conform to their vision of what is right and desirable. From a Christian perspective, the morals and values transmitted as a part of that social reformation are untenable.

What the television elite describe as "realistic," the born-again believer would describe as "reprehensible."

It is ironic that the primary source of oversight in such matters—the government—has vowed to abstain from the battle over what programming is considered permissible. The Federal Communications Commission, which regulates the broadcast industry, has indicated through its chairman (Mark Fowler) that it will continue to take a hands-off approach to the regulation of programming (except in unusual circumstances). Representatives of the FCC assert that "broadcasters have the exclusive right to determine broadcast content," citing First Amendment freedoms of speech as the foundation of their philosophy.[12]

Wired for Action:
The Onslaught of Cable Television

Believe it or not, cable television is neither a "child of the sixties," nor an innovation of the seventies. Cable can trace its modest beginnings back to 1948 in the town of Astoria, Oregon. Wiring together three households with a master antenna located on a nearby mountain, cable was borne under the name Community Antenna Television (CATV). The impetus behind this development was poor reception of network programming caused by interference due to mountains blocking broadcast signals, and the distance from the point of origin of the broadcast signal. As such, CATV was conceived as an alternative delivery system. By strategic placement of a master antenna and subsequently carrying the broadcast signal from that anten-

na directly into a cable subscriber's home, clear reception of all three networks was obtained.[13]

Despite technological advances in signal delivery, cable TV remained a little known phenomenon until recently. Between 1950 and 1960, cable services sprung up in many out-of-the-way towns and villages; yet by 1960 only 650,000 of the nation's fifty-five million households were wired. Despite rapid growth throughout the sixties, there were still only 4.5 million homes served by cable at the start of 1970—a huge jump in just one decade, but still representing less than 10 percent of the homes in the nation. It wasn't until the midseventies that cable started to grow by leaps and bounds. During the seventies, cable penetration tripled; 18.7 million homes had cable service by 1980, which was one out of every four homes in the country. By the beginning of 1984, that figure had climbed to 33 million homes.[14]

A new concept and new technology paved the way for cable's recent explosion in popularity. Technological breakthroughs such as satellite and microwave signal transmission permitted easy access into previously inaccessible homes.

The major breakthrough, though, was primarily a marketing triumph. Rather than looking at cable as a unique means of delivering a broadcast signal, several innovators championed the notion of making cable a programming alternative to the networks. By providing programs that satisfied highly specific interests of TV viewers, cable was able to carve a significant new niche in the broadcast arena. Special cable program services such as Home Box Office (uncut, uncensored movies), Entertainment and Sports Network (round-the-clock sports coverage), Cable News Network (twenty-four-hour news), and CBN (a Christian network) attracted viewers who were searching for an alternative to the material available from ABC, CBS, and NBC.

This new approach to the marketing of cable television caught fire quickly. Today there are more than forty different program services carried by over sixty-two hundred different cable systems operating in fifteen thousand communities throughout the U.S. Cable programming is now received by 40 percent of the nation's homes.[15] Some $9.4 billion has already been invested in the cable industry, resulting in annual operating revenues of $6.2 billion.[16]

The expansion of cable has been so rapid and so firm that another fledgling television delivery system— known as subscription television—has been virtually knocked out of existence. Just a few years ago (before cable caught on) people were touting the prospects of subscription, which offers cablelike programming but transmits scrambled signals that are decoded at the receiving end, rather than pure signals carried over wires. In 1983 subscription television suffered its first loss in total subscribers, dropping to just 900,000 homes nationwide. As cable proliferates, subscription TV will continue to fade. Most experts attribute the collapse of subscription to its inability to offer the multichannel, diverse programming that has lifted cable to its present heights.[17]

Christians, although openly searching for an option to network offerings, have thus far accepted cable with some hesitation. At the end of 1983, non-Christians were almost 20 percent more likely to have subscribed to cable than Christians. Perhaps the major reason behind this disparity concerns Christians' lesser interest in cable's biggest selling point—uncut feature movies. Two-thirds of the non-Christian public who receive cable service claimed to subscribe to at least one movie channel; barely half of the Christians receiving cable made the same claim.[18]

Survey data suggest, however, that Christians are not the morally pure group that many would like to believe. One of the many services available on cable is "adult-only" programming—fare such as X-rated movies and other explicit sexually oriented material. Twenty-three percent of the Christian households wired for cable receive adult-only programming. In this regard, the Christian community is almost indistinguishable from the non-Christian.[19]

One of the most revealing statistics, however, concerns cable loyalty. Network executives have argued that although millions of homes have cable capability, people's program preference remains network shows. There is a growing body of evidence to refute such claims. Among cable subscribers, three out of five people said they spent half or more of their total television viewing time watching cable programs; one out of five cable subscribers said they watch cable programming almost exclusively.[20]

Partially owing to the limited penetration and partially to the continued allegiance to network shows, the networks do continue to reap about three-quarters of the total prime-time television audience. However, this represents a significant slip from the years past, before cable made its inroads (and before public and independent stations also cut into the network share). This trend is evident during daytime programming as well; in 1980-1982, the network share of the weekday morning audience wilted from 73 percent to 65 percent. This shift is undoubtedly related to the prevailing belief that the quality of network programming is on a downward slide. Despite the network's denials regarding audience erosion, the message is loud and clear; people are so frustrated by the programming offered by the networks that they will pay for viewing alternatives. The significance of this development should not be missed. In a time when mounting financial pressures have reduced the average family's disposable income, millions of households are voluntarily spending several hundred dollars per year for services similar to those available to them at no charge.[21]

Christian Television
Christians have a distinctly separate set of options available on both regular and cable television. Relatively few Christians are apparently satisfied or interested in these options, though.

Weekly syndicated religious programs featuring popular evangelists are the most consistently and widely watched Christian programs. There are sixty-six ministries currently seen on television screens across the nation, with dozens more local religious programs (generally church services) available for local viewing only. Despite the crowded field, a handful of the syndicated evangelists have garnered the lion's share of the attention—and audience.

The astounding fact is that despite relatively small audiences, many of these ministries have built themselves into multimillion dollar programs. Each of the ten most watched preachers raises more than $20 million annually from their television followers—and all from a base of support evolving from programs with ratings that rarely exceed a "2" (which means only 2 percent of the total television households in the market were watching). As Table 4.3 notes, the major evangelists have extensive weekly coverage throughout the nation. Most airings are on network affiliates and independent stations, primarily on Sunday mornings.

Analysts have found that there is substantial overlap within the regular total audience for syndicated religious programming. While the most optimistic estimates have run as high as one hundred and thirty million viewers per week, more reasonable estimates fall within the seven to ten million range. This represents roughly one-quarter of the total national Christian population. Ministry claims aside, research has shown that those who are already religiously inclined constitute the bulk of the regular audience; people who have not accepted the basic tenets of evangelical Christianity are comparatively infrequent viewers of religious programming.[22]

Apart from the weekly showings of syndicated religious programs, there are seventy-nine noncable stations across the country that function solely for the purpose of broadcasting religious programming. Generally small-budget operations relying upon extensive use of syndicated religious shows, many of these stations are on the less desirable UHF band (channels 14-83) and only a handful earn any significant ratings. The average Christian station receives a "1" rating or less. By way of comparison, network affiliates (i.e., local stations that carry network programming during prime time) typically generate prime-time ratings between 10 and 25.

Table 4.3

**Audience Data for the Most
Popular Syndicated Religious Programs**

Evangelist	Number of Markets Shown In	Estimated Households Who Watched, Weekly (in thousands)	Estimated Persons Who Watched, Weekly (in thousands)
Richard DeHaan	160	759	1043
Robert Schuller	164	1528	2153
Jim Bakker	152	414	543
Jack Van Impe	86	237	387
Jimmy Swaggart	196	1537	2396
Kenneth Copeland	133	405	591
Jerry Falwell	189	721	1037
Oral Roberts	202	1585	2420
Rex Humbard	152	1050	1586
Pat Robertson	103	408	484

Source: Analysis by American Resource Bureau of data from A. C. Nielsen Company, *Report on Syndicated Programs, Volume 2: Devotional Programs*, February 1983.

Several of the Christian media ministries have chosen to give cable a try. There are three dominant Christian networks carried on cable systems around the country. The largest is the Christian Broadcast Network (CBN), operated by evangelist Pat Robertson (host of the "700 Club"). The PTL Network, under the direction of evangelist Jim Bakker, and the Trinity Broadcast Network, fronted by Jan and Paul Crouch, are the other major Christian cable networks.

CBN is currently received in over twenty-three million of the thirty-three million cable-receiving homes. By comparison, Home Box Office (HBO), the best-known cable network, is available in only 12.5 million households, although HBO subscribers pay a monthly fee for its programs, while CBN is delivered free. CBN is experimenting with variety programming in the hope of gaining a family audience—and loyalty. Top-rated programs on CBN, according to available estimates, have been watched by two million households. The reach of the other Christian networks is considerably smaller. Again, for comparative purposes, a top-rated network program will be seen in fourteen million homes; a well-received cable program could attract four million homes.

Many Christian leaders are interested in how well CBN will do with its variety format. Past complaints about religious programming have centered on the frequent contribution appeals, overly emotional performance of the evangelist, and the similarity of message and presentation among evangelists and even from program to program within a given ministry.[23]

Satellites and Communication
For many years, satellites were space-age instruments used by scientists for measuring weather patterns, glo-

bal dimensions, and other scientific matters. It was not until recently that satellites emerged as a major communications link. As much as any other medium, satellites have the opportunity to alter the face of Christianity in America.

Much attention has been focused on the use of satellites for broadcasting television programs directly to people's homes. Rather than get involved with cable hookups, people would buy a satellite receiving dish and take in various signals directly from the orbiting transponder.

United Satellite Communications, Inc. (USCI) is the most prolific pioneer in this new market, and is aggressively seeking subscribers in communities not served by cable systems. Their package includes twenty-four-hour programming on five channels, which offer news, sports, movies, and other entertainment. People can either purchase receiving equipment ($750 for the satellite dish plus a $25 monthly fee) or rent the equipment ($300 onetime installation fee plus a $40 monthly charge).

Commonly referred to a DBS (for direct broadcast satellite), USCI hopes to enlist 2.3 million homes by 1988, although less than 100,000 households currently utilize DBS. Even with these optimistic projections, USCI is not viewed as a short-term threat to the momentum achieved by the cable industry.[24]

The more interesting applications of satellite transmission revolve around churches and parachurch ministries.

During the past two years, several thousand congregations have joined associations of churches that are receiving satellite-delivered programs designed for use by the church. Some of those ad hoc networks include:

- Church Satellite Network, a growing association of churches in the Assembly of God. There are one hundred churches involved in this network to date.

- Satellite Television Network, operated by the Church of God (Cleveland, Tennessee), and involving one hundred member churches.

- Wesleyan Satellite Network, which encompasses churches affiliated with the United Methodist denomination, and has an annual operating budget of $2.4 million.

- Six hundred and five bodies within the Church of the Latter Day Saints (Mormons).

- Word of Faith Satellite Network, emanating from Robert Tilton's Word of Faith Church in Texas. There are more than one thousand churches associated with this network.

- Catholic Telecommunications Network of America, which began in 1981 and has provided live coverage of the national bishops convention and will also provide a series of seminars on the church and social issues.

- Baptist TelNet, a new service available to churches affiliated with the Southern Baptist Convention. With equipment costs in the $4000-$10,000 range, plus a monthly programming fee that fluctuates according to church membership size, this network has promised four hundred hours of new programming each year.

In addition, there are other denominations that have dabbled in satellite broadcasting with favorable reactions. The Southern Baptist Convention is also introducing a service for home reception, called ACTS (American Christian Television System). That service is slated to provide programming sixteen hours per day, as yet another television alternative for households.[25]

A recent survey by American Resource Bureau found that while church leaders are generally open to the use of new technology within the church, the key to longevity is going to be the quality of the programming offered to churches, whether the delivery system is by satellite or pony express. While satellite systems are off to a fast start in the church market, many churches are cautiously awaiting the early returns to determine if satellite networks will truly energize their ministries via challenging and informative programs, or simply drain the church's financial reserves without a return on their investment.[26]

A similar application has been used by parachurch ministries and independent evangelists. Employing two-way audio and video transmission, these users have found that satellites provide a means of reaching hundreds of thousands of people in an interactive situation that has produced unexpected benefits in education and fund-raising. In less than two years the following "success stories" have occurred:

- Evangelist Kenneth Copeland sponsored a worldwide communion service, tying together the one hundred thousand member congregation of Rev. Paul Chao in

Korea with six hundred and fifty thousand participants located throughout one hundred and eighty American cities and eighteen foreign cities.

- Campus Crusade, the California-based ministry led by Bill Bright, used this technology to raise funds for its graduate university in San Diego. On the evening of the transmission, one thousand six hundred and twenty invited guests gathered in twenty-three cities and pledged five million dollars in donations. The cost of the program to Campus Crusade was only $250,000.

- CBN, Pat Robertson's cable television network, expanded on the Campus Crusade experience, inviting one hundred and sixty-five thousand supporters to a special satellite event. Dispersed across two hundred and seventeen cities in the U.S. and seven more in Canada, CBN collected $6.5 million that evening, against program costs of $950,000.

- In December 1983, the Presbyterian church sponsored a six-hour event in which two thousand of the church's leaders and adherents from thirty-six locations discussed economic justice issues. Spokesmen for the church described the event as "a modern-day town meeting."

- Oral Roberts, one of the pioneers in television evangelism, has used satellite teleconferencing with favorable results. In an ambitious marketing effort, Roberts held a satellite "healing service," reaching two hundred sites in the U.S. and a handful of foreign areas. Later that day, Roberts held a concert and promotional event for junior and senior high school students. In addition to the music, attendees saw a thirty-minute promotional film about Oral Roberts University.

Encouraged by this initial string of successes, many have increased their plans for using satellites in fund-raising and evangelism. Perhaps the most challenging plan yet is in the works for Campus Crusade. Scheduled for December 1985, Crusade is planning to transmit a live event to one hundred foreign locations over five consecutive days. Titled the "World Student Congress," Crusade is projecting a total attendance of one million participants.[27]

The willingness of church leaders to experiment with and embrace new technology has surprised many who dismissed the church as antiquated and close-minded. The early eagerness of these progressive churchmen, however, is not a guarantee that the new satellite systems will have a long-term, long-lasting effect on Christianity in this country. After a glitter of the new machinery wears thin, the true value of satellite delivery systems will be better judged.

The Silver Screen:
Stretching the Boundaries of Taste
For the movie industry, the years immediately following World War II were an unparalleled success. Each year during that period, Americans bought four billion theater tickets. Things have never been the same since.

Media analysts confidently predicted a slimmed-down movie industry in the eighties due to the tremendous expansion of cable television and videotape recorders. As is frequently the case, the "experts" were stunned by the recent upswing in theater attendance. 1983 proved to be the best year in recent history, witnessing a 17 percent increase in tickets sold since 1980. The 1.2 billion sales represented total box office receipts of $3.7 billion.[28]

While Christians have focused the brunt of their attention on television programming, the content of major motion pictures deserves careful scrutiny as well. Many people forget that there was a time when movie ratings were deemed unnecessary. The Motion Picture Association of America, which provides movie ratings, did not commence that process until 1969, largely in response to the concerns of many parents and religious groups that young children were being innocently exposed to detailed sexual acts and graphic violence. Since the advent of the ratings, comparatively little fuss has been raised about what the film industry is producing.

Two significant trends have emerged over the past fifteen years. First, movie makers are releasing fewer films these days. More importantly, the content of the films they are producing is increasingly objectionable from a moral perspective.

As the figures in Table 4.4 point out, there were ninety-nine fewer new films released in 1983 than there were in 1969. A major reason is the dramatic rise in production costs that has occurred over the last fifteen years. It is not uncommon for a major motion picture today to cost the studios in excess of $20 million. There are a handful of top-rated actors who will not even consider a movie project that awards them less than $1,000,000 for their efforts.

The figures also show that the G-rated picture is

the dinosaur of the industry; R-rated movies are the
new bread-and-butter. This represents a reversal of the
way it used to be. In 1969, there were one hundred and
forty-one G-rated films, compared to one hundred and
three R-rated releases. In 1983 the positions were
switched, but with a tremendously disproportionate
imbalance: two hundred and one new releases earned
an R-rating, while only twelve G-rated pictures made it
to the theaters. In fact, R-rated films have grown such
that they represented a solid majority of the new
films—three out of every five releases.

Table 4.4

**Ratings of Newly Released
Movies, From 1969-1983.**

Rating	Percent of total films rated, by year					Qualifying Releases	
	1969	1970	1975	1980	1983	1969	1983
G[a]	32%	20%	13%	4%	3%	141	12
PG[b]	39	35	35	39	39	172	133
R[c]	23	37	48	47	59	103	201
X[d]	6	8	4	10	N/A	25	N/A
Total releases	441	443	425	321	342	441	342

Source: "Decade—High Ratings Tally," *Daily Variety,* November 9,
1983, pp. 7, 34.

[a]General—no age restrictions.

[b]Parent Guidance—no age restrictions, but guidance of parents recommended.

[c]Restricted—no one under 17 admitted without parent or guardian.

[d]Adult—no one under 17 admitted.

Again we find that the personal backgrounds and
values of the major writers, producers, and directors in
the movie industry bear little resemblance to that of the

audience. Table 4.5 shows that the industry is dominated by white males who are wealthy, highly educated, and politically liberal. This profile is very similar to that of the television elite. Even their religious characteristics are equivalent: predominantly of Jewish upbringing, but not currently affiliated or involved with any organized religion.

Table 4.5

**Background Characteristics of
Movie Executives Compared to
the American Public**

Characteristic	Movie Executives	American Public
Male	99%	48%
White	99	87
Raised Jewish	62	2
College graduate	63	24
Earn $200,000 or more per year	64	1
Politically liberal	66	14
Attend church regularly	4	55
No religious affiliation	55	10

Sources: S. Robert Lichter and Stanley Rothman, "What Are Moviemakers Made Of?", *Public Opinion,* December/January 1984, pp. 14-18.

Lifestyle Trends in America, survey by American Resource Bureau, Wheaton, Illinois, 1983.

The values held by these people are similar to those of the television elite—and, therefore, at odds with the values taught in the Bible.

- 96 percent stated that a woman has the right to decide whether or not to have an abortion.

- Only one in four movie executives (28 percent) stated that homosexuality was wrong.

- Three out of five (59 percent) did not feel that adultery was wrong.

Further, movie executives joined their television counterparts in the beliefs that television should be used to promote social reform; that television is not overly critical of traditional values; and that there is not an overemphasis on sex in television programming.[29] In view of these facts, it is not difficult to understand why the attitudes, values, and lifestyles portrayed in movies have changed so significantly in a relatively short time span.

One response from the Christian community has been a feeble attempt to construct its own film production mechanism. The largest producer of Christian films is Worldwide Pictures, a division of the Billy Graham ministry. Combined with the handful of other Christian film companies, the annual output rarely exceeds a dozen full-length films, and the majority of those are intended for use within churches. The most successful Christian films to date pale in comparison to what the secular studios are able to achieve. A decade ago *The Hiding Place* was seen by an estimated twelve million people. *Joni* attracted a theater audience of six to eight million persons, while *The Cross and the Switchblade* pulled in some eight to ten million viewers. By contrast, *E.T.—The Extra-Terrestial* and *Star Wars* have each played to more than fifty million people.

Reading: The Elite Medium

One of the greatest limitations in American society is illiteracy. Much fanfare is made of our educational system and how many millions of individuals have gone beyond high school to receive a college education. Few people discuss the other side of the coin—the massive degree of illiteracy that plagues the U.S. An investigation by the Ford Foundation determined that one out of every three American adults—sixty million people—are either totally or functionally illiterate. A report by the U.S. Department of Education claimed that the figure is actually higher—seventy-two million illiterates.

One of the common measures of literacy is book sales per capita. Compared to other nations, the United States is embarrassingly low on the list, ranking twenty-fourth. Jonathan Kozol, who has studied the problem intensely, claims that illiteracy in America is three times that in the Soviet Union, and five times higher than in Cuba.[30]

It may be surprising, then, to note the substantial growth in book sales recorded in the U.S. during the past decade. From 1970-1980, book revenues skyrocketed from $2.9 billion to $7 billion, an increase of 141 percent. The growth pattern has continued since 1980, with sales nearing the $9 billion mark in 1983.

Religious books, too, have increased their sales significantly, although they remain but a fraction of the aggregate. In 1963, religious books accounted for $81 million in sales, which was just less than 5 percent of the total book market. The early and midseventies, a period of declining interest in religion, saw sales increase to $155 million in 1975, but shrink to just 4 percent of the total market share. The late seventies and early eighties have brought on a resurgence of interest in religion. As a result, religious books more than doubled their sales volume between 1975-1980 and regained their former 5 percent niche of the total market. Currently religious books account for more than $400 million annually.

One of the reasons for this growth—besides renewed interest in spiritual matters—is the increase in the number of Christian bookstores. There are now more than seven thousand such outlets scattered throughout the land, and in 1983 their total sales volume eclipsed the $1 billion mark. Books comprised the major share of that total, but received significant assistance from items such as record albums and tapes, greeting cards, jewelry, and gift items.

It is estimated that about fifty million Americans read religious books, other than the Bible, over the course of a year. Christians, not surprisingly, are more likely to spend time reading such books. A recent survey found that two out of three born-again people (68 percent) had read at least one religious book during the preceding twelve months, while only 15 percent of the non-Christian public had read one or more religious books. Despite the proportional imbalance, these figures indicate that there are nearly twenty million non-Christians engaged in religious reading.[31]

The prognosis is not as sanguine regarding the proliferation of Christian magazines. As a medium, magazines remain popular among all segments of society. In fact, 70 percent of the nation's adults subscribe to (or regularly read) one or more magazines. This is true among both Christians and non-Christians.

However, relatively few Christians have shown interest in publications geared to the Christian audience. It is estimated that less than 5 percent of the Christian public is reached through Christian magazines. The top-rated independent Christian journal does not rate among the top two hundred and fifty publications in the nation. Clearly, reaching a large Christian audience through magazines is best accomplished by the secular magazines. Indeed, it appears that more Christians read the nation's most widely circulated magazine— *Reader's Digest*—than read all of the independent Christian periodicals put together![32]

Drawing the Line:
Enough Is Enough
Given the profound influence of the media on cultural norms and individual behavior, along with the clear admonitions of the Bible to reject that which is impure and improper, Christians have a responsibility with regard to the media. Although some believers have advocated that Christians isolate themselves from the existing media, such an approach is neither practical nor intelligent. Indeed, attempts to create a self-sustaining and self-sufficient Christian media environment have resulted in extensive disinterest among the body of believers.

To date, Christians have achieved a very limited

professional presence in the media industry. Christian colleges and universities have largely ignored the media as a ministry field for graduates and have produced few believers who are qualified to assume meaningful duties within the secular media system. Lacking adequate credentials, relatively few Christians have been able to infiltrate the ranks of the media leadership, thus leaving policy and programming decisions to a group whose values and purposes are of dubious merit. If the media are to be changed, Christians must be willing to "pay the dues" and begin to change things from the inside out.

One of the greatest challenges resides within the creative side of the media. Television, in particular, is a medium that has a voracious appetite for creative products. Each network broadcasts nearly nine thousand hours of programming each year, placing a tremendous strain on the creative process. Conceiving and executing novel, interesting, and intelligent shows is difficult work. But for the Christian trying to gain entry into the system, this represents a significant opportunity. Programming that meets needs—that is, shows that will strike a resonant chord within the hearts and minds of the viewing audience—will succeed.

Perhaps no one in the TV industry understands this principle better than Norman Lear. The creator of numerous network hit series, such as "All in the Family," "Maude," and "The Jeffersons," Lear bases his creative efforts on the development of programs that address the needs and emotions of viewers. Lear provided insight into his creative philosophy:

Now, it's only 1984, but when they start, in '88 and '89, to look back on the '80s, my guess is that they will have everything in the world to do with the need people are feeling for connection and belonging. I think that accounts for the tremendous proliferation of TV evangelicals and all the things we read about of spiritual movements of one kind or another. . . . Entertainment is in the attitudes and feelings and passions of people as they relate to each other.[33]

The select few who have attained "winner" status in the mercurial world of Hollywood production—such as Lear and Larry Gelbart—have demonstrated that the chances of affecting an audience are enhanced by designing messages that acknowledge and deal with the condition of the audience in a realistic fashion.

Too often, however, television is subject to the perspective typified by Seth Abraham, vice-president of programming at Home Box Office:

The boundaries of good taste change over time, and what may be unfashionable today may be fashionable tomorrow. Americans' taste in everything—not just television—is constantly evolving.[34]

For the Christian involved in the media, whether as a professional participant in the process or a member of the audience, such a relativistic viewpoint is untenable. Christianity is not an evolving set of moral and ethical standards shaped by the whims of the marketplace. While Paul's message in 1 Corinthians 9:19-23 recommends the value of adaptability in communication and presentation, the gospel plainly teaches that there are boundaries as to what is right and wrong.

But how can Christians who are outside of the secular media maze, for whatever reasons, have an impact?

The Christian media certainly represent a possible means of affecting people's lives for Christ. We can learn from the secular elite some of the important principles in mass communications and apply them to the Christian media, without automatically accepting the bankrupt values from which they sprang.

For instance, in becoming more sophisticated about audience needs, leaders in the Christian media should make greater use of market research. Secular media groups use research to identify the needs and interests of the audience; to define the niche which the media organization fills in people's lives; and to evaluate how successfully the organization is achieving its objectives.

Christian media organizations would also benefit from setting—and living up to—higher standards of performance. Too often, Christian magazines allow strong graphics to compensate for weak content. Christian television stations are notorious for poor production values and unimaginative programming, despite potentially explosive content.

Effective marketing is another downfall of many Christian media. Literally millions of Christians are unaware that Christian magazines, as a category, even exist. Similarly, Christian TV stations rarely concern themselves with their image among the audience, failing to realize that a bad image (whether deserved or not) will seriously impede the station's chances for reaching people.

Christian stations might also find it profitable to reevaluate their very method of operation. As things stand now, stations sell time rather than buy programming. This is at least partially responsible for the mediocre quality of much of what is seen on Christian TV. The secular networks formerly ran their affairs similarly, before discovering how much more efficient it was to rely upon independent producers for new material. Many of the financial woes now common to the religious outlets could be alleviated by following the networks' change of course.

Every Christian, as a television viewer, has a responsibility relative to the media. Believers must wake up and accept television, in particular, for what it is—not what they are told it is.

Careful scrutiny should be applied to the entertainment values and news reporting perspectives promoted on television. When improprieties are found, remedial action should be taken. For instance, people should express their feelings about immoral programming to the networks and to their local stations. Products sold by the commercial sponsors of such programs should be boycotted and letters of explanation forwarded to those sponsors. Involvement with "watchdog" groups, such as the Coalition for Better Television—whether it be prayer, volunteering, or financial support—is another vital step.

Parents have a unique set of media responsibilities. Surveys indicate that few parents oversee the amount or type of TV programming consumed by their children. Efforts to judiciously monitor and regulate such viewing are in order. Parents should also assess their family's TV diet. When watching television becomes the family's dominant source of togetherness, changes may be necessary to restore more constructive forms of relationship and interaction. Other forms of media monitoring—such as checking the types of magazines and books read by children—should also be undertaken by parents.

Many adults—Christian and otherwise—have already succumbed to the glitter of new media technologies. Followers of Christ, however, have an obligation to carefully evaluate the media alternatives facing them. Many are tempted to embrace media that offer "state-of-the-art" delivery or novel programming. Prior to making such commitments, the substance of what is to be delivered should be closely examined to be certain that the messages received will exert the kind of influences on lifestyle and behavior that are consistent with scriptural admonitions to abstain from all evil.

5 Moral Majority or Mild Minority? Christians in Politics and Community Affairs

The study of political behavior has become an obsession with the American public. The media emphasize political events in their reporting; people continually debate matters of public policy and politics; literally billions of dollars are spent in political activity. The magnitude of our political interest and involvement renders America unique in the world.

Many would argue that the degree of political interest and involvement of Americans is attributable to the fact that the United States is a "model" democracy. Pluralism—the free and unabated exchange of independent ideas and competing points of view—has flourished in this country as in no other society in modern times.

Yet, in spite of the international acclaim our system of government has received, during the last five years that system has come under attack from within. A coalition of politically conservative Christians, often referred to as the "New Religious Right," has challenged the widely held assumption that pluralism is alive and well in America. Jerry Falwell and the Moral Majority (among others) rose to prominence in 1980 on the strength of the contention that the Christian perspective—the very perspective upon which this nation was founded—has been consistently denied a fair shake by our nation's leaders over the past several decades. Although the furor created by these conservative religious activists has often eclipsed the significance of the issues and elections which fueled their emergence, the persistence of the New Religious Right has raised public consciousness in this area, and has begun to have an effect on the nation's political agenda.

Losing the Faith

In seventeenth- and eighteenth-century America it would have been inconceivable to suggest that this nation be governed without a central Christian influence on both policy-making and the conduct of government. The belief that the Bible provides direction in every area of life was one of the key elements of the Reformation which was translated into early American political thought and practice. The influence of a Christian world view is evident in the Constitution, as well as in the recorded statements of many of our early leaders (such as Jefferson and Madison). Even as late as 1840 the renowned French analyst of American society, Alexis de Tocqueville, wrote:

> Christianity has retained a strong hold on the public mind in America; its sway is not only that of a philo-

sophical doctrine which has been adopted upon inquiry, but of a religion which is believed without discussion. . . . In the United States, Christianity itself is an established and irresistible fact, which no one undertakes either to attack or to defend. The Americans, having admitted the principal doctrines of the Christian religion without inquiry, are obliged to accept in like manner a great number of moral truths originating in it and connected with it.[1]

De Tocqueville was greatly impressed by Americans and the quality of their lives. In his view, America's freedom and progress was a direct outcome of the public's single-minded agreement on and acceptance of the principles of Christian faith.

Toward the end of the nineteenth century, however, the American lifestyle began to change significantly. Christianity began to lose its place as the cornerstone of public decision-making.

Ironically, it was the ascension of a religious movement—pietism—that pushed the nation in a new direction. Pietism was a form of Christianity in which a person's salvation was regarded as a highly personal experience. The pietist movement tended to separate religious experience from the debate and formation of public policy. As the pietist movement matured, more and more Christians turned their focus inward and championed the clear-cut distinction between the spiritual and the worldly.[2]

At the same time the pietists were making waves, Darwin broadened the attack on the traditional Christian value system by expounding his theory on the evolution of mankind. During this transition period, a growing number of government leaders assumed a secularized world view.

As if Christianity (as a socio-spiritual philosophy) was not going through enough trials already, the combined force of previously unparalleled social change, post-Civil War animosities and dissension, and the secularization of public leadership resulted in a serious theological split within the Protestant community. In reaction to the new social developments (e.g., urbanization, large-scale immigration, "scientific" study of religion, communications technology that led to radio broadcasting and telephones), a brand of "liberal" Protestantism emerged. While the more conservative Protestants waged a continuing battle to redirect Protestant churches to more traditional concerns, the widespread diversion of attention away from grass-roots political matters further weakened the role of Christianity in government.[3]

The Environment Continues to Change
Until very recently, the trend in American government was toward the centralization of power. The federal government, largely at the expense of state and local ruling bodies, obtained broader jurisdiction and authority. Today, however, a reversal of the power pendulum is underway. Government is becoming increasingly decentralized, as local and state governments are winning back greater authority in policy matters. The expansion of state and local power has been actively supported by the actions of the Reagan administration.

In addition, although American government has typically operated as a "representative" democracy, it is subtly shifting to a "participatory" form of government. Rather than relying upon elected officials to do their bidding for them, Americans are getting more directly involved in the political process. Examples of this renewed commitment include:

- Declining voter turnout for federal elections, and increasing turnout for local elections.

- Broadening popularity of referenda and initiatives, in which voters actually mandate policy.

- Increased levels of interest (e.g., issue discussion and concern) and involvement (e.g., campaign involvement, petition signing) in the political process on the local level among thousands of people who previously avoided such involvement.

Yet another major shift in the way our government is running concerns the new tact required for survival in political America: coalition building. In days past, policy victories were achieved by establishing majorities based upon party loyalty or personality strengths, rather than upon the merit of legislation. Today the traditional bases of support are fragmented. Party loyalty is considered antiquated and unsophisticated. Single-issue advocacy groups abound. The electorate is becoming increasingly segmented according to ideological and issue orientation rather than demographic correlates. As a result of these changes, passage of legislation often necessitates a temporary, opportunistic association of minority power blocs.

While the new rules in government and politics suggest that Christians, as a minority power, have the opportunity to regain some of their lost clout in affairs of state, the politically oriented attitudes and behavior of the Christian body indicate that the opportunity will most likely be neglected.

The Role and Political Behavior of Individual Christians

Some political observers have cautioned that born-again Christians are becoming more politically aware and active. They fear that Christians, representing a different sociopolitical philosophy, may come to dominate or substantially alter the political landscape.

There are some data to support the claim that Christians are becoming increasingly politicized in concert with their religious convictions.

- An increasing percentage of Christians claim that they would be more likely to vote for a candidate if they knew the candidate was also a born-again Christian. The percentage jumped from 42 percent of the Christians who were registered to vote in 1980, to 53 percent in 1983.[4]

- By a wide margin, Christians are more likely to say that they are informed about the religious beliefs of the candidates they vote for than are non-Christians. The figures are 53 percent and 32 percent respectively.[5]

- Christians are in general agreement and exhibit high-opinion intensity on issues that have a clear religious orientation, such as abortion, prayer in public schools, and teaching the creation theory.[6]

- Christians are somewhat more likely than non-believers to state that their attitudes and feelings make a difference in society.[7]

These findings suggest that the Christian community is becoming increasingly sensitive to the relationship between their faith and matters of public policy.

However, there is a more revealing set of statistics to indicate that Christians, as a group, will not be among the political "movers and shakers" in the coming decade. Although Christians have increased in attitudinal awareness, there is no discernible increase in their intent to act upon those attitudes. As students of politics know, attitudes are important; but attitudes not supported by action lack power.

There are three primary reasons why Christians will not play an active role in the unfolding political drama of this nation. The first two reasons are:

- *Complacency.* To their credit, Christians are more satisfied with the nature and quality of their lives than are their non-Christian counterparts. For instance, relatively more Christians were found to be "very happy" with their community (64 percent—55 percent). The born-again public was also more likely to report often feeling happy about their life (82 percent—67 percent). With comparatively little sense of discomfort with their lives, Christians will have less motivation to sacrifice their free time and get involved in political activities.[8]

- *Chronic inactivity.* Christians have a recent history of being followers rather than leaders. Only one out of every five Christians (20 percent) contends that he frequently participates in political activities. Even fewer—only one out of twenty-five believers, or 4 percent—has ever run for a public office. Even in voting turnout, Christians are not distinct from non-Christians. Grass-roots activities such as writing to elected officials and petition-signing are also not likely to characterize Christians (except perhaps in those cases involving issues deemed inflammatory by many believers, such as abortion). Given this record of inactivity—which is especially unnerving considering that our past three Presidents have identified themselves as born-again, and labored to make the Capitol's climate more amenable to a Christian world view—there is little reason to suspect that this Mild Minority will emerge from the closet to forge a significant political machine in the near future.[9]

The third reason Christians are not expected to make waves politically has to do with an ongoing transformation in the American population that has been picking up steam for over a decade: the population redistribution. America is an unusually mobile society. Long gone are the days when sons and daughters were almost certain to spend their lives in the town where their parents raised them. The phrase *home town* has almost ceased to have a meaningful place in our vocabulary. These days, the average family lives in a community for no more than five years.[10] America has become a nation of gypsies.

The 1980 Census drove home the reality of our mobility. For the first time in the nation's history, more people lived in the South and West than in the Northeast and Central states.[11] This shift is significant to Christians because it means their political strength—

which has always been heavily concentrated in the South and Southwest states—will be diluted. Many of those who are trading belts—that is, leaving the "Frost Belt" for the so-called "Bible Belt"—are not Christians. This is especially true of emigrants from the Northeast. The overall effect of this southward movement will be to diminish the influence of Christians by reducing their percentage of the total vote, thereby rendering the Christian constituency less potent.[12]

Christians in Public Office
The bad news for Christian activists is that there is no reason to suspect that there will be an increase in the number of Christians elected to public office. The complacency of Christian voters and the relative lack of enthusiasm toward personal political activism are largely to blame. The dilution of the Christian vote brought about by population shifts will also hurt. From the politician's point of view, considering that the born-again public constitutes only 30 percent of the adult population—the Mild Minority—Christianity cannot be viewed as much of an asset on the campaign trail. Even the majority of Christian voters admit that a candidate's spiritual leanings are but one of a myriad of credentials that they carefully weigh before selecting a candidate.

The good news for Christians is that there is less and less "closet Christianity" in public leadership. While politics may not be enticing a great number of Christians to become involved, the believers currently in public office are noticeably less timid about their faith than were many of their predecessors. The efforts of Presidents Carter and Reagan have been instrumental in altering the environment in Washington in such a way that it is no longer embarrassing to admit being a Christian to one's legislative colleagues. In fact, one study of Congressmen concluded that, contrary to the prevailing myth, the five hundred and thirty-five members of the House and Senate are every bit as religious as the people who elected them—and probably more so.

A study conducted by the Search Institute consisted of in-depth interviews with a random sample of Congressmen. Among the key findings of the study were:

- 95 percent believed in God, the same proportion as among the general public.[13]

- Two out of three (71 percent) affirmed the divinity of Jesus Christ. That is nearly identical to the level measured among the general public (69 percent).[14]

- Congressmen were somewhat less likely to regularly attend church services than were their constituents: whereas 45 percent of the general public typically attends a church service at least weekly, only 32 percent of the Congressmen interviewed were equally diligent.[15]

- Like the public, about seven out of ten Congressmen pray on at least a weekly basis, although fewer of them (compared to the public) pray on a daily basis (45 percent, against 57 percent of the total population).[16]

- The same proportion of Congress and the American public are born-again Christians—30 percent.[17]

While these statistics are a long way from suggesting that the nation's halls of political power have been overrun by a league of saints, neither do they wholly condemn the Congress as a fortress of atheists and agnostics. The study further pointed out that roughly one-quarter of our Congressmen have a "total commitment" to religion in their lives and jobs; about half have a "moderate commitment"; and the remaining one-quarter have a "casual commitment." This parallels with amazing accuracy the nature of the people who elected those officials.[18]

Bridging the gap between the elected and the electorate are Christian advocacy groups. The presence of a Christian world view is being increasingly felt in Washington through the heightened involvement of Christian lobbying groups and qualified Christians who provide "expert testimony" at Congressional committee hearings. In the past several years, for instance, Christians who have been called upon to offer expert opinions on pending legislation include James Dobson and his collegues with the Family Research Council; John Whitehead and his legal partners at the Rutherford Institute; and Robert Dugan and his staff from the National Association of Evangelical's Office of Public Affairs.[19] Intensified lobbying efforts are one outgrowth of the 137 percent increase (between 1970 and 1980) in the number of Christian lobbying groups on the Hill. Most of that growth has occurred among politically conservative Christian organizations, which ballooned by 325 percent, compared to a 58 percent growth rate among liberal Christian groups.[20]

The Institutional Church in Politics

Little credible research has been conducted regarding recent efforts of evangelical churches in the political life of the country. A reading of the related literature, however, reveals that this is an area of considerable controversy: should the institutional church be active in politics or not?

Perhaps the dominant perspective among Christian practitioners, theologians, and scholars regarding the political responsibilities of the church could be summarized as follows:

- The institutional church should not become involved in political matters as an ongoing political power broker or force. The result would be a division among Christians. Nonbelievers could interpret church involvement as condoning the world's value system and power structure, and as an attempt to make inroads and gain influence in that system.

- One of the chief duties of the church is to educate Christians. This responsibility encompasses Christian political involvement. The political education provided by the church should seek to accomplish two ends. First, Christians must be informed of the political situation and of the appropriate scriptural response to such conditions. Second, the church must motivate Christians to exercise their right and responsibility as American citizens to play an active role in public and community affairs. While it would be counterproductive for the church to be consistently engaged in political struggles, many church leaders and Christian political observers identify community involvement through individual Christians as an obligation of the church.

- The church, as a body, does have a mission to those in need. It is a mission that has been neglected, resulting in government usurpation of the authority to meet those needs (welfare, emergency medical care and shelter, food provision, etc.). The church must reestablish its role in this regard.

Achieving these ends will take some dramatic changes in church policies and in the attitudes of churchgoing Christians. "Churches and religious groups" rank near the bottom of the list of those who Christians think will produce our future political leaders (only "the media" ranked lower). Note, on the other hand, that survey data show Christians to be more open than non-Christians to becoming more active in community and politicial affairs.[21] It could well be that Christians are just waiting for someone to show them how to translate their spiritual beliefs into a practical social and political philosophy and lifestyle.

Opportunities and Obstacles

The eighties and beyond hold tremendous political opportunities for Christians if they are willing to capitalize upon those opportunities. Some sweeping shifts in philosophy and practice must occur, though, before the born-again community is likely to make its presence felt in a large way.

Perhaps the largest burden is on the back of the institutional church. First, there is the doctrinal hurdle: should the leaders of God's people encourage believers to dive into politics? Even if the answer is affirmative, nurturing political leaders will be an uphill struggle. Pastors and other church leaders will have to familiarize themselves with an entirely new area of investigation, and will have to reflect more deeply on the relationship between Jesus' teachings and contemporary world events. Leaders will then have to communicate their perspective to believers in a manner that will educate, prepare, and motivate the flock for meaningful social action.

In the process, the church must also decide whether it will continue to deny its social welfare responsibilities. If caring for the downtrodden is an accepted duty of the church, new tracks must be laid to enable the church to carry out these obligations.

The flow of useful political information must be increased, and that information must flow to both leaders and followers. Currently, information on political issues and public policies is largely collected by single-issue groups or lobbying groups. They channel their findings, interpretations, and recommendations to the political leadership of the federal, state, and (sometimes) local governments. One of the reasons why Christians, as a group, have no political "bite" is that the core whose views these lobbyists and other activities are supposed to represent—the fifty million born-again Christians—infrequently receive the benefit of the same information that is given to political leaders. The result is a poorly informed and complacent constituency. Eventually the inert nature of that constituency will undermine the political clout of those who represent their views and thereby strengthen the position of those advocating a secular political view.

The quantity and quality of information being provided for government leaders could also be increased. Because of the rapidity of change occurring in our society, and the backlog of problems that legislators and other public leaders are expected to handle, those leaders are faced with the need to make more decisions than ever, and to make them more quickly than was expected previously. One Congressman stated that the philosophy of that body is that "it is better to make bad decisions than to make no decisions on matters of importance." It is precisely because of that pressure-cooker environment that Christians have a heightened responsibility to provide government officials with persuasive and reliable insight on the issues. If, as was stated earlier, our society is unique because pluralism flourishes, Christians must be certain that their interests are not disregarded simply because they did not take the time or make the effort to add their perspective to the competition. If government officials are overburdened, it would be foolish to assume that even Christians involved in government would always be able to find the time to independently arrive at a "Christian" response to a given issue or situation.

Along these lines, if Christians put aside many of

the petty doctrinal differences that divide them, a Christian "think tank" could be inaugurated (a group of scholars and researchers whose sole function is to conceptualize and analyze problems and move toward the development of policy solutions and evaluations). The Congress, state legislatures, and the media (who greatly impact the behavior of local leaders) are strongly moved by the conclusions of secular think tanks— the Brookings Institute, American Enterprise Institute, The Rand Corporation, the Hudson Institute, etc. By bringing together Christians who could synthesize sharp critical analysis of our social and political problems with an understanding of scriptural mandates to the leadership of a nation, a credible and tremendously useful resource would be operating for God's glory in the midst of secular influences. Such a group would also centralize much of the information-gathering that needs to take place if forceful arguments are to be presented on behalf of America's Christians.

A final consideration is: the people. "Politics is people," bumper stickers read, and indeed, without mass involvement a democracy loses its vitality. Unfortunately, barring some unforeseen, cataclysmic event, Christians are likely to continue to wallow in political apathy and lethargy.

Earlier it was suggested that complacency, chronic inactivity, and dilution of power will minimize the Christian political presence in the years ahead. But there seems to be a fundamental problem that has long been overlooked and which urgently needs to be addressed. Christians, as a rule, do not possess political philosophies that transcend the superficial. Lacking such a unifying perspective, every issue and social occurrence is viewed as an isolated incident. In reality, though, no issue exists in a vacuum. But without an overall philosophy of Christian political concern, believers are unlikely to interpret events within the context of "the big picture." Their impact will be small because their vision is small.

If Christians are to influence society for Christ, it cannot be done through a shotgun approach to morality, justice, and righteousness. Christian leaders must acknowledge and fulfill their responsibility to move the Christian community toward a political philosophy that is consistent with the teachings of the Bible. But before that can take place, a significant number of individuals who profess Christ as their Savior must recognize the emptiness within their own lives and witness. Coming to grips with this deficiency will require determination and perseverance. If Christians are to accept the challenge presented by James and his fellow-disciples that we must live what we preach, then understanding how to live and how to encourage others to live in obedience to God's command is central.[22]

Last—but never least—is the importance of prayer. Through the petitions of God's people, great things can come to pass. Only one out of four Christians claimed to frequently pray for our public leaders, and only one in three admitted to praying often for events taking place in the world.[23] Certainly not every person is cut out for a life of political activism, but there is no Christian who can live a meaningful life without a prayerful relationship with God. Those prayers should include matters of public policy and conduct. This is one way in which every Christian should be active in politics.

6 The Litmus Test of Faith: Personal Spiritual Commitment

The dictionary defines *commitment* as "being obligated or pledged to a specific position or undertaking." Personal commitment is the source from which truly Christian behavior springs—faithful people obligating themselves to a mentality and lifestyle that conforms to the ways of life called for by Jesus and spelled out in the Bible.

It is an undeniable fact of modern life that commitment to a Christian perspective and lifestyle is made difficult by the numerous interests that compete for people's time, energy, and intellect, and by the reality that we are limited in the number of substantial obligatons we can fulfill. While the Bible acknowledges the attraction of worldly events and beliefs, the second chapter of James forcefully states that absolute commitment to the life, death, and teachings of Jesus is of unparalleled importance. James went so far as to warn readers that the failure to demonstrate faith in Jesus through daily behavior renders such faith meaningless.

The extreme diversity of activity that occurs within Christians' lives provides countless opportunities to employ the principles of faith. Whether it be a word of encouragement to the downcast, or a silent, sincere prayer to the Creator, each passing day presents new ways to glorify God through our behavior.

The thrust of this chapter is toward examining the spiritual commitment of the born-again population. To better understand where Christians are in their level of commitment to the gospel, indicators to be examined are primarily those that are overtly associated with growing in faith: attitudes about the importance of religion; involvement in Bible reading, prayer, evangelism; financial support of the church; etc. If the Christian body is to have an indelible impact on society, individual Christians must demonstrate their willingness and diligence to expand their personal understanding of their faith, and the adoption of the tenets of that faith into their lifestyle.

The Importance of Religion

Modern America has gone through a radical change in its attitude toward religion. During the fifties and early sixties, about three out of four people felt that religion was "very important" in their lives. From the midsixties through the late seventies, the perceived significance of religion plummeted. By 1978, only one out of two people stated that religion held a "very important" place in his life.[1] Sociologists have developed dozens of theories related to this revised outlook, many of which focus on the liberalization of social attitudes. This new moral and ethical code has led to the widespread acceptance of "contemporary lifestyles"—a type of "anything goes" philosophy that operates in opposition to the practical boundaries established by Christian beliefs.

The late seventies put the brakes on the trend toward minimizing the personal importance of religion. Gallup surveys indicate that 1978 may have been the turning-point; at that time, 52 percent of the public felt religion was "very important" in their lives. The figure inched upward to 55 percent in 1980, 56 percent in 1981, and remained at 56 percent in 1982.[2] The significance of these figures is not so much that they are crawling upward, as that they suggest that the twenty-year downward spiral has been arrested.

Born-again believers, as would be expected, have been more highly influenced by religion than nonbelievers. Although the available figures point to stable attitudes regarding the impact of religion on the lives of born-again believers since the midsixties, recent Gallup studies show that religion has assumed a slightly greater importance in the lives of Christians too. In 1978, 76 percent of the Christian public stated that religion was "very important" to them, and the figure rose to 81 percent in 1980 and 82 percent in 1982.[3] To provide a comparative standard, consider that when Christians were matched against non-Christians on this item, the figures were 76 percent versus 38 percent in 1978, and 81 percent versus 39 percent in 1980. Put differently, Christians were twice as likely to regard religion as an integral part of their lives.

The Size of the Christian Body and Prospects for Growth

The substantial amount of attention focused by the media on the Christian population could easily give the impression that the born-again public is multiplying by leaps and bounds. The fact that people in general are embracing an increasingly favorable attitude toward religion and its influence in daily situations indicates that the social climate is fertile for such growth.

Perhaps the environment is ripe, but available data do not support the growth theory. Over the past seven years, roughly 30 percent of the American public have been classified as born-again Christians.[4] Proportionally, there has been no real growth. Numerically, because the national adult population has increased from one hundred and forty-five million to one hundred and seventy million since 1976, the total number of born-again Christians has risen from forty-five million to fifty-three million. In other words, it is only because the national adult population has grown by 17 percent over the past seven years that the Christian public, too, has increased its following by 17 percent. There has been no percentage gain; 31 percent of the public was born again in 1976, and 31 percent of the current population is born again. Christianity is merely keeping up with where it has been for quite some time.

Perhaps the most disturbing misinterpretation of current spiritual conditions concerns the claim of some prominent evangelists that America is undergoing a massive spiritual revival. It depends on how *revival* is defined. If gains in church attendance, more positive attitudes about the importance of religion in one's life, and any demonstration of belief in Jesus are to be construed as the unmistakable signs of a revival, then America is experiencing such a transformation. If, however, revival is to be understood as a broad-based, radical departure from the ways of the world—a deep-rooted commitment to Jesus Christ and the principles he taught, as manifested in the daily activities and thoughts of committed believers—then America may be only on the threshhold of revival. By this latter definition, America is not yet immersed in a national revival.

Much of the confusion may stem from the methods used to determine religious commitment as the indicator of revival. Indeed, the percentage of people who claim to have made a personal commitment to Jesus Christ that is important in their lives jumped from 53 percent in 1980 to 64 percent in 1983.[5] That represents an impressive increase in just three years. Deeper digging, however, reveals that among the 64 percent who claim to have made such a commitment, only half believe that they will obtain eternal salvation because Jesus Christ died for their sins. The other half—who cannot truly be considered born again—cite various works that they are performing as their ticket to Heaven.[6]

What the nation is experiencing, then, is not an encouraging explosion in saved souls; rather, there is a tremendous hunger for true faith being demonstrated by the public. An entire generation was raised without the benefit of substantial religious training or reflection. Other values and opportunities were substituted for a spiritual foundation. Plagued by nagging feelings of personal inadequacy and lack of self-fulfillment, millions of these people have turned to religion to determine whether or not it can help bridge some of the gaps in their lives.

Yet, in spite of the hundreds of millions of dollars spent on television and radio evangelism, the millions of Christian tracts and books distributed annually, and the ubiquity of churches and born-again believers, millions of Americans are hearing only a part of the gospel. While the openness of these searching individuals to the way of Jesus is promising, their desire for honest spirituality has not been served adequately by the local Christian body. What America is witnessing is not so much a revival as the initial preparation of people's hearts and minds for a revival.

The Myth of the Meek Christian
The media have proven very successful in stereotyping Christians as little old ladies living out their days in rural poverty in the Southern states. The figures presented in Table 6.1 show that such a caricature is grossly misleading. For instance, compare the facts to the stereotype:

- Females do, in fact, make up the majority of the Christian body, representing roughly three out of every five believers. However, that leaves some twenty-two million males involved in the Christian family.

- The elderly are only slightly more likely than their juniors to have made a personal decision for Christ. Because people over sixty-five comprise only one-seventh of the total adult population, the elderly represent the smallest segment within the born-again constituency. Altogether, about one in six Christians (16 percent) is elderly—not quite nine million of the fifty million believers. Young adults—the "under 35" group that is so frequently chided for ignoring spiritual matters—are, in fact, the people least likely to make a Christian commitment (only one in four have done so). But their large numbers in the general population mean that they contribute almost seventeen million Christians—one out of every three Christians. Adults in the middle age ranges—from thirty-five to sixty-five—compose the majority of Christianity, with people in the forty-five to sixty range the most prolific.

• Christianity has taken a bum rap regarding the educational background of its adherents. Two-thirds of the adult public have a high school diploma or less—exactly the same ratio found among the Christian public. Even the division among the one-third who have attended college—that is, half of those attended but did not graduate, and half graduated—is identical between the Christian and non-Christian populations. Thus, while it is true that most Christians are not college educated, that statement is no less true for the American population as a whole.

• Sociologists have learned that personal income tends to increase with educational attainment. Given that relationship and the above data regarding the parallel educational achievements of the Christian and non-Christian communities, it should not be surprising that the income distribution among Christian and non-Christian households is indistinguishable. In 1983, about half of the public was earning less than $20,000 annually, and half was earning above that level—regardless of their spiritual convictions.

- There is a considerable regional disparity that cuts across religious ties. Christians are less likely to be located in Northeastern and Far West states than are non-Christians. The difference is made up in the South and Southwest. While just 29 percent of the U.S. population live there, 41 percent of the Christian public call that area home.[7]

Table 6.1
Profile of the Christian Population

Characteristic	National Population Percent of total	National Population Millions of people	Born-Again Population Percent of total	Born-Again Population Millions of people
All adults	100%	170.0	100%	52.7
Sex: Male	48%	81.6	42%	22.1
Female	52%	88.4	58%	30.6
Age: Under 35	39%	66.3	31%	16.3
35-65	47%	79.9	53%	27.9
Over 65	14%	23.8	16%	8.4
Income: under $20,000	52%	88.4	53%	27.9
$20,000-$40,000	41%	69.7	40%	21.1
over $40,000	7%	11.9	7%	3.7
Education:				
high school or less	69%	117.3	69%	36.4
some college	15%	25.5	14%	7.4
college graduate	16%	27.2	17%	9.0
Region:				
Northeast/Mid-Atlantic	26%	44.2	16%	8.4
South/Southwest	29%	49.3	41%	21.6
Central	27%	45.9	29%	15.3
Pacific/Mountain	18%	30.6	14%	7.4

Sources: U.S. Department of Labor, Bureau of Labor Statistics, 1983 population estimates.

American Resource Bureau research studies, conducted November and December, 1983.

What this amounts to is that the media have fooled the public into believing that Christianity is the solace of a powerless, downtrodden, futureless minority. The Christian community, in reality, is a vibrant and contemporary segment of American society, a slice of the population that encompasses all types of people and that closely resembles, in many ways, the national public to which they belong.

Living with the Bible

One behavior that should clearly distinguish Christians from the rest of society is their involvement with and knowledge of the Bible. As the blueprint for a righteous and holy existence, the Bible should emerge as the most important document in the life of Christians.

A tiny percentage of the born-again segment (2 percent) maintain that the Bible is neither the literal nor inspired Word of God. Two-thirds of the Christian body believe that it is the actual Word of God and is completely true. The remaining one-third hold that it is the inspired Word, but is not to be interpreted literally. This is a substantially different perspective than that assumed by the general public, which is about equally divided as to whether the Bible is the inspired or literal Word of God.[8]

The significance of the Bible in the lives of believers appears to be growing fairly rapidly. The frequency with which people read the Bible has risen from 39 percent in 1978 who said they read it at least several times a week, to 53 percent who were equally diligent in 1983. Participation in small-group Bible studies—

not including Sunday school classes—has been rising steadily during the past five years to the point where three in ten Christians are currently active in such a group.[9]

These favorable indicators are balanced, however, by some disturbing realizations about the apparent value that Christians derive from the Bible. For openers, Christians devote a relatively limited amount of time to reading the Bible. In an average sitting, Christians spend about twenty-four minutes reading Scripture. Over the course of an average week, figuring in the frequency with which believers read the Bible, the typical born-again person spends about sixty-eight minutes reading the Bible. As an act of commitment, Bible reading is dwarfed by endeavors such as watching television, reading newspapers and magazines, spending time with friends, engaging in personal hygiene activities, and commuting. If a list of all weekly activities was compiled and the devotion to Bible reading among Christians was assessed, it would rank as a low priority.[10]

The relatively small amount of time that Christians allocate to Bible reading helps to explain why there is such a deficiency in Bible knowledge. Several years ago George Gallup discovered that less than half of the born-again community could list five of the Ten Commandments.[11] More recently, Gallup found that only three out of five Christians could recall the names of the first four books of the New Testament, and only half of the Christians interviewed correctly identified Jesus as the person who delivered the Sermon on the Mount.[12]

Overall, then, while Christians claim that the Bible is their main material source of guidance, they devote relatively little effort to becoming familiar with its contents. The recent surge in Bible study participation lends some hope that Christians are recognizing their limitations in the area of biblical scholarship and are taking corrective steps. While it is too early to contend that this reaction is a blossoming trend—the resurgence is too recent to characterize it as a significant, large-scale departure from biblical illiteracy—America may be on the verge of a renewed and widespread interest in scriptural knowledge and understanding.

A Review of Other Forms of Spiritual Commitment
The evidence regarding spiritual activity beyond Bible reading intimates that the constant admonitions of Christian leaders are falling on deaf ears. Some of the most common routines of the Spirit-filled Christian life are missing from the lives of a large portion of the born-again public, and there seems to be no movement toward adopting those fundamental practices.

Prayer may be the area in which Christians are closest to "getting their act together." If assessed by the regularity with which Christians engage in it, prayer is a relatively universal, routine act. Four out of five Christians say that they pray at least once each day. Over the past five years, there has been no perceptible change in the proportion of Christians who pray on a daily basis.[13]

As for prayer content, Christians' prayers are startlingly similar to prayers offered by non-Christians.[14] When asked to describe the concerns they always include in their prayers, the response was as follows:

Table 6.2
Content of Christian vs. Non-Christian Prayers

Items "always" included in prayer	Christians	Non-Christians
Thank God for what you have	90%	73%
People you know	74%	58%
Your own spiritual growth	71%	52%
Your health	66%	61%
Things going on in the world	31%	31%
Guidance for public leaders	28%	19%
Material things that you want or need	7%	7%

In the area of contributing money to support church and parachurch operations, Christians are markedly more generous than non-Christians, but fall short of upholding the scriptural command to tithe their income. Again, the evidence shows that there has been virtually no change in the behavior of Christians during the past five years. In 1978, one in three Christians (34 percent) claimed to give at least 10 percent of their household income to the church; in 1983, that figure held steady (32 percent). Incredibly, one out of five Christians indicated that they give no money to the church. While a portion of that group are elderly people who are living off meager fixed incomes, the majority of the group have no such excuse.[15]

The weakest link in the lives of many Christians is, by their own admission, personal evangelism. Survey after survey shows that the one thing Christians feel least capable of doing is sharing their faith with nonbelievers. It is surprising, in light of this proclaimed failure, that Christians have remained as persistent as they have in trying to communicate their beliefs. Four out of five Christians have attempted to witness to others in the past, and half of the born-again public makes an attempt at witnessing in any given month.[16]

This diligence is a reflection of the value Christians place on the gospel, and a measure of the seriousness with which they regard the Great Commission. Half of the born-again public considers sharing their beliefs with the unsaved to be "very important"; nine out of ten Christians believe it is at least "somewhat" important.

The rub comes regarding Christians' self-image in the evangelism process. Only one out of every twelve believers—8 percent—feel that they usually have a substantial influence on the beliefs of the people with whom they share. Concurrently, surveys in several evangelical churches have found that despite believers' dissatisfaction with their ability to share the gospel with nonbelievers, members of those congregations were more interested in receiving guidance in areas germane to their own spiritual development and lifestyles (such as developing greater self-discipline, enhancing their self-esteem, and controlling their emotions) than in receiving training in evangelism techniques.[17]

While this may seem contradictory—i.e., that

people believe in witnessing and feel ill-prepared for the task, yet have little desire for the church to nurture them in that area of weakness—it is not. One of the major deficiencies of the church is its inability to translate the gospel into practical steps for daily living. Combining the perceived inability of the church to develop a meaningful course of action for evangelism, and people's anemically low sense of self-esteem, there is little wonder that Christians express comparatively little interest in gaining new skills for evangelism. Already hurting in self-confidence and self-image, believers are less than enthusiastic about receiving training that, judging by past experience, is likely to earn them additional rejection and abuse. How ironic it is that the church, whose function it is to edify the faithful and prepare them to renew the world for the sake of Christ, is seen by its own supporters as incapable of providing those people with the confidence and skills they need to claim victory for the Kingdom.

Promise in the Midst of Disappointment

In evaluating the spiritual condition of American Christians, it is difficult to suppress the temptation to warn that Christians are not sufficiently committed to their faith. Such an argument is safe, for it is unlikely that believers in this society would ever reach a saturation point in commitment to Christ. There is always room for improvement.

Despite that caution, a strong case could be presented to demonstrate that this nation's born-again public must intensify its level of commitment to Jesus. Literally millions of born-again people are consistently negligent in fulfilling their responsibilities to God. One out of five does not bother to pray during the course of the average day. (That's ten million Christians who will give their Creator and Savior the silent treatment today.) Two out of three hoard their money, refusing to return to God the tithe. During the next thirty days only one out of every two Christians will tell a nonbeliever about the joy and comfort that comes from knowing Jesus personally, and most of those will retreat from the experience feeling frustrated by their inability to effectively communicate their very reason for living. Proponents of lifestyle evangelism must shudder upon realizing that some twenty-five million Christians are incapable of consciously conforming their lives to the guidance of the Ten Commandments simply because they do not know what those commandments are. Indeed, improvements could be made.

Commitment, as defined earlier, is the devotion of oneself to a specific task or entity. Commitment implies motivation, and it appears that this is where the system breaks down for Christians. Many born-again people want faith to be easy. They are not interested in hearing about (much less experiencing!) the suffering that following Jesus may demand, or the diligence required in study of the Scriptures or the seeking of God's will, or the material sacrifices that are expected of those who are devoted to Jesus. Phrases that motivate the bodybuilder, like "no strain, no gain," are anathema to many Christians. They will remain spiritually committed as long as the path to righteousness is not too demanding.

But commitment is only a piece of the problem. Just as importantly, the church as a body has lost its ability to communicate. Many Christians have redefined communication as a one-way process—giving information. This twisted definition of communication has infected the church to the point where it often cannot effectively help itself. Everyone is talking, but no one is listening. Christians have been reaching out to one another, crying for help in some very specific areas of personal hurt and individual ministry. Too often the responses have provided satisfaction to the sender rather than to the receiver of the message.

In spite of the shortcomings of Christian ministry—or perhaps because of those failures—the remaining fifteen years of this century hold tremendous revival potential. It is an exciting time because there is the potential for heightened enthusiasm and growth in the commitment of existing believers, along with the possibility of attracting millions of those who are aimlessly seeking meaning in life and are open to the chance that religion could provide some answers. There is a voracious public appetite for practical spiritual insight. It is up to the entire body of believers to accept the challenge and satisfy that spiritual hunger.

7 The Church:
The Corporate Context
of Christianity

Christianity encompasses elements of collective and individual spirituality. As a collective phenomenon, aspects such as denominational affiliation and church attendance are most commonly studied. However, there is certainly more to understanding the nature and being of the aggregate Christian church than these two factors.

In this chapter, data are presented regarding the vitality of corporate Christianity—that is, the church as a collective entity. These findings should be regarded in tandem with those presented in the accompanying chapter on the individual spirituality of the American born-again population. Indeed, concentrating on the collective experience without concurrently examining the character and intensity of Christians' personal spiritual lives would result in an incomplete and misleading perspective on Christianity. In reality, each is inseparable from the other. For analytic reasons, studying the individual and group elements of Christianity will clarify some of the changes taking place in America's religious behavior and values. In reading this chapter, it should be kept in mind that the term *born again* refers to a perception on the part of those claiming a born-again experience, not a judgment by the authors as to whether or not a born-again experience has actually occurred.

The Early Church
In the New Testament, which ultimately is the source to which one should go to understand the beginnings of the Christian church, the term *church* referred not to a building or place, but to a meeting or congregation of Christians. The early church, then, was simply a group of people who willingly came together to share certain beliefs and customs that they held to be an important part of their existence. Some of the customs and traditions outlined by various references in the New Testament include:

- Belief in Jesus Christ as the risen Messiah, one who was sent by God to redeem his people.

- Regular corporate worship, generally at a synagogue.

- The baptism of those who believed in Jesus as the Messiah, done in the name of Jesus.

- Fellowship among believers, which included common meals and prayer, usually in the homes of believers.

- Adherence to the law, which was seen as a necessary but insufficient (for salvation) aspect of Christian faith.[1]

While much attention is focused on the church of Jerusalem, many scholars argue that the true model of the modern Christian church evolved in Antioch. Under the leadership of Barnabas, that branch blossomed through the diligent evangelistic efforts of early missionaries and through the establishment of new local ministries and church bodies. There was no hierarchy or formal structure in the church during this early period, though the seeds of hierarchical development were present in that the apostles had responsibility for overseeing the churches they had founded. But this still left room for a great deal of independence and autonomy in local congregations, and strict lines of authority were absent from the early church.

The religious history of the United States indicates just how far corporate Christianity has strayed from its roots. Today there are more than one hundred and seventy distinct religious bodies in this country, and at least sixty of those could be considered evangelical. The level of control and conformity exercised by denominations within affiliated churches ranges from a highly structured, authoritarian approach to virtually unrestrained independence. The practices and beliefs that were standard in the early church have remained central to some denominations, have been reformed to serve as a theoretical launching pad in others, and have become anathema to still others.

Growth and Decline in Christian Bodies
Examining trends in denominational growth and decline is a starting-point in the study of the institutional

church. The figures in Table 1 show the relative size of the largest Christian-oriented denominations. During the past decade, the denominations whose membership has grown the most include Baptist, Church of God, Assembly of God, and Nazarene churches. Some denominations considered outside the orthodox Christian framework have enjoyed similarly rapid growth, most notably in the Mormon and Jehovah's Witness fellowships. The largest losses have occurred among churches affiliated with the Presbyterian, Lutheran, and United Church of Christ denominations.[2]

Table 7.1
Membership in Protestant Denominations, 1982

Denomination	Number of Churches	Total Members	Members/ Church
Baptist	94,805	27,053,617	285
Methodist	51,909	14,187,266	273
Lutheran	18,203	8,487,012	466
Presbyterian	14,979	3,481,618	232
Episcopal	7,215	2,786,004	386
Church of Christ	17,000	2,500,000	147
Pentecostal	23,817	2,277,261	96
United Church of Christ	6,443	1,726,535	268
Disciples of Christ	4,295	1,177,984	274
Church of the Nazarene	4,888	492,203	101
Church of God	4,775	292,444	61
Mennonite	2,210	255,438	116
Brethren	2,665	290,982	109
Christian & Missionary Alliance	1,436	195,042	136
Wesleyan	1,789	108,904	61

Source: World Almanac, 1982, pp. 352, 353.

In keeping with the focus of this book, however, the most pertinent data relates to the denominational affiliations of born-again Christians. It turns out that the denominational membership distribution assumes a different shape when the born-again experience is the qualifying factor.[3] The distribution is as follows:

Table 7.2
Distribution of Born-Again Christians by Denomination

Denomination	Percent	Members
Baptist	32%	16,000,000
Catholic	12%	6,000,000
Methodist	10%	5,000,000
Presbyterian	7%	3,500,000
Lutheran	7%	3,500,000
Episcopal	2%	1,000,000
Nondenominational, independent	7%	3,500,000
Other	23%	11,500,000

(Adjacent to the percentage of the born-again population who associate with each denomination is the approximate number of born-again Christians affiliated with the denomination.)

Two observations of particular interest can be drawn from these statistics. First, notice how many born-again Christians are worshiping outside "mainline" Protestant churches—42 percent, or better than two out of every five Christians. To put this in context, remember that the mainline denominations encompass nearly three-quarters (72 percent) of the Protestants in this country. That is significantly more than the 58 percent of the born-again public who align themselves with mainline churches.[4]

Second, many evangelical Protestants will be surprised by the large number of Catholics who are born again. Proportionally, few people within the Roman Catholic Church describe their Christian experience in terms of having personally accepted Jesus as their Savior—one in six Catholics. However, because the Catholic population of America is so large—fifty-two million adherents—they constitute 12 percent of the entire born-again community, a total of six million people. That gives Catholics the second largest number of persons claiming to be born again among all denominations.

What will happen to the denominational mix among born-again church affiliates? Projecting church growth is a complex task, involving a number of factors that the denominations rarely measure. Academicians have had only limited success at developing reliable ways of predicting church growth.[5]

Despite the weaknesses in current methods, the data available suggest that more and more Christians will align themselves with independent, nondenominational churches. While denominational churches will continue to dominate the field—over the next decade independent congregations will likely account for no more than 15 percent of the total born-again community—the mainline bodies will continue to lose ground.

This probability is consistent with other expected shifts in the lifestyles of Christians: the preference for participatory forms of government; the quest for personalization in the work place; increasing involvement in individual sports at the expense of team sports; more favorable attitudes toward small companies; the continued preference for a nonurban environment; and the like. These are expressions of freedom and individuality. Worshiping at a church that is not tied to a distant,

impersonal, hierarchical authority structure comple-
ments those expressions.

Along the same lines, expect to see a shift to
smaller congregations. This has already begun to take
place. Many Christians are desperate for friendships
with their spiritual kinfolk. For thousands of Christians, the anonymity and feeling of insignificance that
often results from being part of a large congregation
hinders or precludes the development of meaningful
personal relationships with other believers. Many people interviewed in opinion surveys have indicated their
willingness to sacrifice first-rate preaching and Sunday
school teaching for the opportunity to develop deep
and lasting bonds with other Christians. Many of those
people believe that smaller congregations are more likely to present such opportunities.[6]

As a result of the mobility of the American household unit, America's population is being redistributed
between regions. As the population shifts, the church
life of literally millions of people will be disrupted and
new beginnings made. This will contribute to the reshaping of the denominational map.

Church Attendance

Thus far this discussion has overlooked a crucial item:
church attendance. All the denominational trappings
and church buildings in the world won't matter if no-
body turns out to worship on Sunday mornings.

Here a distinction needs to be made between denominational affiliation and church attendance. Affili-

ation concerns an individual's personal identification with a religious body. Attendance connotes participation in church functions, such as worship services. Many Americans identify with specific denominations but feel no particular obligation or responsibility to be active in a church associated with that denomination.[7]

The levels of church attendance among Christians have been quite stable since the late seventies (when researchers first started identifying and evaluating the born-again community). Today two out of three Christians attend a church worship service on a weekly basis, and four out of five attend at least two times each month. This is double the proportion of non-Christians who attend services on a weekly basis.[8]

Attempting to foresee future attendance patterns requires some measure of the value received from services by attendees, in conjunction with a measure of the importance of church attendance to the individual. Better than four out of five Christians believe that church attendance is an important part of their spiritual life.

As for the performance of the churches in fulfilling Christians' need to be part of a significant church body, the results are only moderately reassuring. When Christians who attend a church were asked to describe their feelings about the worship services they normally attend, two-thirds said they usually found the services to be "satisfying" and "educational." Three out of five Christians described the services as "inspiring." Yet, only one-third considered the services to be "challenging," and one-third also called the worship times "predictable."[9]

The implication to be drawn from these data is that Christians want to feel that their worship is "significant," but one-third leave their churches feeling letdown on the average Sunday. The fact that these disappointed Christians continue to attend church is a tribute to their insistence on the importance of worship and being part of a God-glorifying body. However, barely half of those who claim they are generally satisfied by their services would maintain that the services present any meaningful spiritual challenge.

It would be wrong to assert that these ominous signals point to a pending exodus of believers from our churches. If the data were available, it is likely that the same sense of disappointment and yearning for better leadership in worship could be traced throughout the past several decades. In some ways, believers have been conditioned to expect and accept mediocrity in corporate worship. For the most part, their feelings of disappointment and emptiness are based on notions of the ideal, rather than particular in-church experiences.

The upshot of these findings is not so much a threat to the survival of churches—where would truly committed people go?—as much as it offers a fundamental challenge to church leaders to establish worship services and church events that are more meaningful to those who participate. Because of the changes in the distribution of the faithful in coming years due to population shifts, those churches that are able to make worship come alive by lifting the spirits of the flock, pushing them to perfect their own spirituality and truly glorifying God through corporate activities, will be the ones most likely to expand their ministries.

The Minister as Counselor

During the past decade, there has been an increase in the number of people who have sought professional counseling to help them cope with the pressures and problems of their lives. Counseling has become a multi-billion dollar enterprise fragmented by specialists. There are marriage counselors, sex counselors, family counselors; more traditional counselors include psychiatrists, psychologists, and ministers.

Studies by American Resource Bureau have shown that about one-quarter of the public has sought professional help. While ministers rank as the third or fourth most likely choice of all people seeking counseling (psychologists and psychiatrists are the most popular), the majority of people who turn to ministers for help are born-again Christians. In fact, among Christians, ministers were the most popular type of counselor.

Of even greater significance was the finding that Christians were just as likely as non-Christians to have been to a counselor in the past. This is a result of a major shift in people's attitudes about professional counseling. Once deemed an escape route for the weak or demented, nine out of ten Americans, regardless of spiritual convictions, now believe that seeing a professional counselor to help work out personal problems is an acceptable approach.[10]

Generally, people have not been greatly satisfied with their counseling experiences, regardless of the type of counselor they have seen. Only half of those who had been through some counseling rated it as "very effective."

Because our society is changing so rapidly, and because change is one of the realities with which people have the most trouble coping, some experts foresee an increased need for counselors in the coming years. The sweeping revisions that will alter our society will also increase people's reliance upon the perspectives and guidance of objective outsiders. Ministers will be increasingly active in counseling during the next several years.

However, just as word-of-mouth can make-or-break the survival of a church, so will the recounting of the personal feelings and recommendations of Christians who have sought counseling from church staff impact the fate of ministers as counselors. To their credit, many seminaries have upgraded their counseling programs in the past decade, and most now require that every graduate have some training in various areas of counseling. However, unless current and future church leaders can truly minister to the hurts and agonies that their charges are experiencing, both ministerial counseling and the perceived practical value of Christianity will suffer the consequences.

Women in the Church
One of the most controversial areas pertaining to church leadership and growth concerns the role of women. Since 1970, their place in the church has changed dramatically. While some people might argue that the feminist movement that rocked the nation during the late sixties and early seventies left no imprint on the church, available information supports the opposite line of reasoning.

- In 1970, women represented 2 percent of the ministers in this country. Today, while still a small proportion, they have doubled their numbers (4 percent) and are increasing in size every year.[11]

- Fifteen years ago less than 10 percent of the students enrolled in evangelical seminaries were women. By 1977 that figure had risen to 13 percent, and in 1983 women were 16 percent of the population at evangelical seminaries. Such growth is occurring at seminaries that were already leading the way in female enrollment (such as Mennonite Brethren Biblical Seminary, which jumped from 13 percent women in 1977 to 26 percent in 1983), and at seminaries that had severely limited female enrollment, such as Dallas Theological Seminary, which has expanded its female roster from less than 1 percent to 8 percent in the last seven years.[12]

- Despite historically closed attitudes toward women in the ministry, popular thinking on the subject has been reversed. A staggering majority of both Christians (82 percent) and non-Christians (90 percent) now believe that women should be more involved in leadership roles in the church.[13]

While recent events show a decided move toward acceptance of women as full-time, professional church leaders, philosophical and practical struggles are still being waged in this area. The gains won over the past decade by women in ministry roles need to be put in a broader context to understand how far women have yet to go if parity with men is an objective.

- At the start of this decade, there were seventy-six religious bodies that had consented to the ordination of women to the full-time ministry. However, there were eighty-seven religious bodies who did not recognize the ministry as a woman's place.[14]

- Through 1980, the mainline Protestant churches, in particular, offered the fewest opportunities for women. For instance, the percentage of ordained females in those denominations included 0.3 percent in the American Lutheran Church; 0.8 percent in the Episcopal church; 0.7 percent among the Lutheran Church in America; 0.04 percent in the Southern Baptist Convention; 0.9 percent in the United Methodist Church; and 2.1 percent in the United Presbyterian body.[15]

- More than half of all ordained females were from one of three bodies: United Church of Christ, American Baptist Churches, and Disciples of Christ. Pentecostal churches were responsible for one out of every three ordained females.[16]

- While the Christian public believes that women need an expanded part of the church leadership, they are not as keen on allowing them full partnership with men in most prolific and prestigious posts. There was near universal approval of women serving as Sunday school teachers (100 percent), Bible study group leaders (98 percent), field missionaries (98 percent), and members of church boards (90 percent). The harmony dissolves when considering females for delivering sermons (79 percent, which is still relatively strong support), and serving as pastor of the church (62 percent). The most consistent resistance to women preaching and pastoring came from Baptists.

Even when the statistics give reason for encouragement about the expanded role for women, the recounted experiences of many ordained females dampens any welling enthusiasm. Many ordained women are frustrated at not being able to serve to what they believe to be their full capacity due to denominational anxieties about involving women on "the front lines" of ministry. Mainline bodies, especially, have attempted to pacify some of their ordained women with support roles such as hospital visitation and college chaplaincies, rather than involving them in primary roles in local congregations.

The near future will sustain the pattern of slow growth in the number of ordained women and in the levels of responsibility they will be granted. The area in which the greatest degree of progress will likely be made is in terms of female lay leadership. An increasing percentage of board and committee members—deacons, trustees, elders, Christian education—will be female. Representatives of some religious bodies have found this to be a way of satisfying the need to recognize the leadership potential of women and using their gifts without upsetting the male dominance in "professional" leadership. Opportunities for female leadership will be especially acute in churches which are in a state of crisis. In such bodies, every individual who demonstrates concern takes on a relatively elevated importance—regardless of gender. The chains that have bound women to secondary functions in those congregations are more likely to be broken during such times of need.

Roads to Maturity: Attitude and Action

Survival is not the key issue for most churches. For many congregations, the critical consideration is that of attitude.

A prime example is the suspicion of Catholics that many born-again Protestants continue to feel (though it must be admitted that there are misunderstandings on both sides). The fact that Catholics represent the second largest segment within the born-again population should serve as evidence that God works through the hearts and minds of people, not ecclesiastical structures. Recent changes in the Catholic Church—sometimes manifested on the local level, rather than emanating from Rome—may reflect a shift toward a less traditional-based religion and toward a more Spirit-directed faith. Protestant-oriented churches and believers must be open to the spiritual struggle of Catholics, rather than ready to assert their purported spiritual superiority.

A different attitudinal challenge concerns the capacity of churches to anticipate and respond intelligently to change. As churches suffer the loss of members, new strategies will be developed to reestablish the viability of those churches. Congregations that choose to ignore the currents of societal change will render themselves defenseless against deterioration. The churched and unchurched alike indicated that they would welcome a church that is more sensitive to their real needs—not the needs that church leaders imagine they have, or think they ought to have. People today are rebelling against monolithic authority structures. They need to be involved. They need to feel valuable. They have to sense that they have a stake in the direction that their spiritual lives are taking. Churches that remain aloof and designed for observation more than participation will wither.

Perhaps the most important aspect of involvement that churches need to facilitate is fellowship. If Christian leaders could listen (as the authors have) to what people say about their churches, their feelings of alienation from other believers, and their overall loneliness, they would know the necessity of making the church more compassionate and sensitive. Churchgoers agree that they are taking home strong doses of "head knowledge" every week; but relatively few claim that they are warmed by the feeling of belonging to a loving and caring body. A monthly potluck dinner just won't do. The church needs to actively integrate itself into the daily lives and relationships of those who comprise it.

Perhaps, too, the worship services that typify the Christian's Sunday morning experience need to be more challenging. The nature of the challenge is not intellectual, for most people are satisfied with the education they receive on Sundays. In addition to supplying the conduit for friendships to bloom, more attention could be devoted to the practical aspects of Christianity and a lifelike expression of worship to the Creator.

People want to be participants, not just observers; but they want to be involved in activity that is uplifting. Most Christians would describe their Sunday morning experience as a time of "compliance" more than a time of "celebration." If the church cannot spiritually intoxicate its most committed followers, the hope that they will enthusiastically promote their faith to nonbelievers is unfounded.

8 Christianity in America: The Tragedy of Worldliness

Abraham would have appreciated the dilemma of modern America. Some four thousand years ago, when the city of Sodom was facing the destructive wrath of God over the magnitude of its collective sin, Abraham pleaded with God to spare the city if fifty righteous men could be found within the city's confines. God consented. Abraham then asked God if he would demonstrate such mercy if only forty-five righteous men were located. Again God agreed to do so. The conversation continued in like fashion, with Abraham seeking the promise of God's compassion even if only forty, or thirty, or twenty, or ten righteous men were identified. In each instance, God granted that he would spare the many for the sake of the few (Gen. 18:20-32).

Were a modern-day man of God to represent this nation before the heavenly throne, the ensuing conversation would likely be similar to that which Abraham initiated on behalf of Sodom. Although Christians today have gained righteousness in God's eyes through the sacrificial death of Jesus, America would be hard-pressed to locate many genuine followers of Christ.

The practice of American believers has proven that pure Christianity—faith in Jesus that is untainted by the values and treasures of a profane world, as exemplified through beliefs, speech, and conduct—is an ideal, unrealized concept. To some degree, that is natural and expected since Christian doctrine maintains that "no man stands perfect before God." However, numerous indicators suggest that rather than adhering to a Christian philosophy of life that is occasionally tarnished by lapses into infidelity, many Christians are profoundly secularized, and only occasionally do they respond to conditions and situations in a Christian manner. Recent research shows that many Christians are especially vulnerable to the worldly philosophies of materialism, humanism, and hedonism.

The frail and self-serving nature of Christianity in the lives of so many believers is nothing new. Since the time of Jesus' earthly ministry, his followers have struggled to strike a balance between their spiritual walk and their performance in the marketplace. Perhaps at no prior moment in history, however, have so many Christians waged the battle for piety and holiness so lackadaisically and failed so consistently in their quest for righteousness.

The Prophecies of Worldliness

To place the dilemma of practicing Christianity in a pagan environment into perspective, one must return to the teaching of Jesus. Exercising divine wisdom and insight, Jesus foretold the seduction of men by the ways of the world. In the Gospels, Jesus proclaimed that:

- people would deny the importance of consistent righteousness and, as a result, devote their attention to the pleasures of the world, behaving no different than nonbelievers (Matt. 24:45-51; Luke 8:11-14).

- people would adopt a distorted sense of priorities, consistently choosing the pleasures of the world over the calling of God. For instance, Jesus scolded the Pharisees for following the traditions of men rather than the commandments and leading of God. He later told the parable of those who would hear the Word, but whose faith would be diluted by their indulgence in life's riches (Mark 7:6-13; Luke 8:5-15).

- the lust for possessions would prevent many from accepting the spirit of Christianity and, ultimately, from receiving the gift of salvation due to the deification of material objects (Matt. 19:16-22).

- weak faith would cause many people to be ashamed of their God. As a consequence, their faith would be of little value, and would lead God to be ashamed of them (Mark 8:34-38).

- the disparity between righteous words and a sinful lifestyle would betray the heart of many. Jesus berated the Pharisees for being hypocrites—preaching one thing, but doing another (Matt. 23:2-12).

The apostles, following Jesus' example, continued to stress the awareness and rejection of the world's ways. The Apostle Paul was especially persistent in cautioning people against falling to the temptation of the world's evils: love of money, immorality, idolatry, pride, selfishness, drunkenness (see 1 Tim. 6:10; Gal. 5:16-24; Eph. 5:3-5, 18; Rom. 1:18-32).

The banner of "lifestyle Christianity" has since been carried by a long succession of saints. Augustine, in the third and fourth centuries, belittled the Christians of that age for allowing philosophers to elevate the wisdom of man to a position of eminence. Rather than subordinating the human mind and will to that of the Creator, Augustine observed that men treated knowledge as an end in itself, taking false pride in their perceived ability to control all that was real.[1] His "City of God/City of Man" polemic described the contrast between two world orders, and criticized men for repudiating the objectives of the Kingdom of God.[2]

In medieval times, St. Francis of Assisi and St. Thomas a Kempis continued the crusade for a humble servanthood among believers. Society increasingly denigrated or ignored their pleas, however, and by the late Middle Ages corruption and immorality were all that was known to many. After several centuries of continued moral decay, the Reformation emerged, advanced by the likes of John Wycliffe, Martin Luther, and John Calvin. These radicals attacked both the materialistic tendencies of the church, as well as the unrestrained debauchery and perversion of the people. They extolled the virtues of poverty, sobriety, marital fidelity, and sincere spiritual commitment.[3]

In recent times, the exhortation to godliness has lost neither its force nor sense of urgency. Francis Schaeffer has powerfully articulated how America, in particular, has turned its back on Jesus in favor of a credo of humanism. Citing the crumbling moral foundations of the government, education, and the media, Schaeffer has concluded that Christians will lack social influence as long as their lives are self-centered and motivated by greed and worldly success.[4]

Other influential contemporaries have also attempted to shake Christians into awareness. Logically dismantling the philosophy of Carl Sagan, whom he describes as the "dean of American humanists," Clark Pinnock has attacked the empirical bankruptcy of secular humanism. Ron Sider, John White, and Os Guinness have written extensively about Christian rationalization and striving for material wealth. Even secular authors like Christopher Lasch have noted the narcissistic tendencies of our culture.[5]

American Christians:
Americans First, Christians Second
Through the grace of God, America has become a nation of tremendous prosperity. No other nation in the history of the world has known such material abundance, nor enjoyed such a broad distribution of that wealth among its people. In the process, though, America has become a victim of its own progress.

For instance, as an outgrowth of this nation's devotion to material well-being, America has become the world's foremost champion of hedonism. This is a mindset in which the acquisition of pleasure and enjoyment is the highest priority in life. Responsibilities such as worship of a holy God, fulfillment of obligations, and personal improvement are deemed of secondary importance. Having fun is all that counts. The affluence of American society has elevated pleasure-intended activities from the realm of the "desirable" to that of the "essential." An entire sector of the economy has blossomed to satisfy the spectrum of people's urges. America has become a hedonistic heaven.

Concurrently, the secular humanist perspective has gained credibility as a result of social progress and increased prosperity. The development of new technology is largely responsible for the shift from an industrial-based economy to one predicated on the acquisition, analysis, and transmission of knowledge. The resulting concentration on the creative and intellectual capabilities of man has steadily and subtly undermined God's eminence by reinforcing the humanist view that man alone is the center of the world and responsible for its progress.

The naive acceptance of these blessings and strides as being natural for mankind points to the superficiality of many Americans who call themselves Christians. The realization of prosperity has not led to the glorification of God for his faithfulness and graciousness to this nation. On the contrary, the satisfaction received through those gifts has produced a body of believers who laud themselves for engineering such advances in material and physical well-being.

Survey data supply ample evidence of the bankruptcy of the commonly held world views of Christians. It is undeniable that as a body, American Christians have fallen prey to materialism, hedonism, secular humanism, and even to a jaded form of Christianity that rejects much of the commitment required of faithful servants.

A recent national survey discovered that no fewer than seven out of ten Christians are prone to hedonistic attitudes about life.[6] The study found, for example, strong support among Christians for the sixties notion that an individual is free to do whatever pleases him, as long as it does not hurt others. Two out of five Christians maintain that such thinking is proper, thus effectively rejecting the unconditional code of ethics and morality taught in the Bible. A similar proportion of born-again people deny the possibility that pain or suffering could be a means of becoming a better, more mature individual. That, of course, refutes the scriptural teaching that pain and suffering are a means to perfect our faith. As a final example, three out of ten Christians agree that "nothing in life is more important than having fun and being happy." While few theologians or mature Christians would argue that God desires a morose, joyless cadre of believers, the Word of God clearly teaches that the highest values are those of praising God, obeying his commands, and seeking his Kingdom.

Regarding materialism, the statistics are nearly identical. Two out of three Christians express such love for money, possessions, and other material objects that their Christianity cannot be said to rule their hearts. For instance, more than half of the Christian public believes that they "never have enough money to buy what they need"—not what they "want," but what they "need." One out of four believers claim that "the more things you have, the more successful you've been." Not only are these beliefs counter to those expressed in Scripture, but the fact that the proportion of Christians who affirm these values is equivalent to the proportion of non-Christians who hold similar views indicates how meaningless Christianity has been in the lives of millions of professed believers.

Secular humanism, another perspective on the meaning and logical conduct of life, has lately become a controversial topic in Christian theological circles. Indeed, it should be a matter of heated debate, since seven out of ten Christians support at least some of the principles central to the humanist perspective. Attitudes about abortion provide such a clue. The fact that 40 percent of the born-again public believe that there is no right or wrong position on this matter intimates their frivolous, clouded understanding of the sanctity of human life in the eyes of God, and the responsibility that we have to honor God through life. Similarly, 42 percent of the Christians interviewed said that without the government's laws, there would be no real guidelines for people to follow in daily life. When close to half of the Christian body overlook the Bible as an authoritative guideline for society, the restricted relevance of faith and spiritual commitment in people's lives becomes clear.

Given the worldly leanings of believers, it is perhaps not surprising to find that even on purely spiritual matters an appallingly high ratio of Christians stray from the nucleus of their professed faith. One out of five born-again people do not even consider religion to hold a place of great importance in their lives. One in ten assert that many of the values and principles taught in the Bible are outdated and of little practical use. Twenty percent consider the mere possibility of sacrificing their lives for the advancement of Christianity to be out of the question.

Overall, less than 5 percent of the Christians in this nation are not entangled in the deceits of materialism, secular humanism, or hedonism. Some three-quarters of the body of believers are guilty of impropriety in at least two of those philosophic pits.

Preparing for the Future: The Challenge to Christianity
For Christians, the problems are many and the solutions seem few. Indeed, the social changes outlined in preceding chapters will intensify the pressures to which American Christians will be subjected. America will become more and more polarized as material wealth continues to escalate, as leisure time comes to be regarded as a right rather than a privilege and luxury, and as scientific and technological advances showcase the intellectual potential of the human race. As the tensions mount, expect to see a sharp division between the "worldly Christians" and those believers who forsake the gains and pleasures of the world as ends in themselves. In short, it is going to get tougher and tougher to be a true Christian.

Many Christians will respond by ignoring these conditions, with the hope that the tensions will harmlessly fade away. Yet, the severity of the problems facing the faithful cannot be accepted as a valid excuse for delaying a sincere, wholehearted effort to overcome the obstacles to corporate righteousness.

What strategy will most effectively nudge Christians toward the fulfillment of their God-given duties? No human could rightfully claim to possess perfect insight on that matter. However, research and prayerful inference suggest a direction for that pursuit.

The initial step is for Christians to become aware of the problems with their faith and external witness. Problems cannot be righted if those who are in the wrong are ignorant of their condition. In tandem with awareness must come a total comprehension of the problems. Christians must not just pay lip-service to the tragedies of materialism, hedonism, humanism, or shallow Christianity. Understanding must be followed by the earnest desire to right the wrongs, which implies strong remedial action.

Take the example of materialism. Through exposure to sermons and reading, as well as the prompting of the Holy Spirit, most Christians know that materialism is not of God. In fact, 84 percent of the born-again people in this nation believe that "the United States is too materialistic" and should become less so. But these same people do not perceive themselves to be part of the problem; it's a case of "those other Americans" being at fault, not the individual reflecting on the question. Within a matter of seconds, the same Christians who conceptually rejected materialism will express their concern over never having enough money to suit their needs, believing that the quantity of possessions defines the quantity of success they have achieved, and so forth. Christians have deceived themselves into believing that the problem of materialism in this country could be corrected if only those other people would rectify their attitudes and behavior.

This "it's not me" mindset is deeply ingrained in the Christian culture. Partial blame must be directed at Christians' understanding of salvation and its obligations. Many Christians have taken the position that since their salvation is "guaranteed," they have no further responsibility to assimilate the tenets of Christlike behavior into their lifestyle. The assurance of salvation has perverted their sense of enduring obligation to God. For this reason alone, the importance of discipleship in the cultivation of the body cannot be overemphasized.

Leadership has often failed in the past because it has remained too theoretical, getting carried away with doctrinal rambling that has little overt relevance to the average Christian seeking enlightenment for his own daily walk. Thus, it is not enough for Christian leaders just to admit that there is a problem and that they should address it; their approach to the problem must be brutally practical, almost mundane in its pragmatism.

Again, research may be helpful in suggesting some approaches in this regard.

- *The "average Christian" needs role models.* Psychologists have learned that one of the ways that people grow is through the imitation of models. Christians have a disadvantage in this regard. Believers typically are unaware of any contemporary Christian individuals after whom they could pattern their lives; they are ignorant of the models that could be drawn directly from the Bible; or they deem Jesus as the only role model in Scripture whom they should attempt to copy. Hopelessly unable to follow his perfect example, they give up on even trying. To date, when Christians have been asked to identify others who they think lead a highly spiritual, godly life, relatively few names emerge. Those that do surface are often representatives of the professional ministry (e.g., Billy Graham). As a culture, we need to nurture and recognize those who by their lifestyle and conscious effort could assist other believers in leading a Christlike existence. Of course, this needs to be accomplished without diminishing the importance of humility, servanthood, and the primacy of Jesus as our ultimate example.

- *Very simply, Christians must be challenged to increase their commitment to spiritual growth.* Perhaps too often the ministry of the church stresses evangelism at the expense of discipleship. Recent converts and mature believers alike need to continually grow in their spiritual life; stagnation brings spiritual decline. Churches need to take seriously the business of edifying the flock, just as individual believers need to reaffirm their commitment to becoming Christlike. Christian principles must be made practical, with valid applications of those principles a central part of the teaching/learning process.

- *There is a deep-set need for consistent repentance.* Many churches—and consequently, Christians— have put a great distance between their sinful nature and the resulting need for God's continued grace. Repentance and confession must be reestablished as a focal point of people's lives. Such submission and humility could go far toward helping Christians resist the temptations of worldliness.

- *True Christian community may be the most important component of all.* Millions of Christians feel they are waging a solitary battle. Sadly, loneliness is every bit as common among Christians as among the unsaved. The advantages of creating a vibrant community among the born-again public are manifold. Besides the fellowship and encouragement that would result from such bonding, believers would be made accountable to one another in implementing the principles taught by the church and found in Scripture. Failures in belief, conduct, and speech would be identified more consistently and quickly; change could occur more predictably and less painfully.

In the final analysis, there will be no acceptable excuse for Christians not to have revolutionized the world for Jesus' sake. The information available portrays many American Christians as people who are playing a grand game—playing church, playing parenthood, playing social activist, etc. But the turbulence that will transform this nation during the coming two decades is not part of any game. If we, as Christians, are to be a light in the darkness, it is time we flip the switch "on" and illuminate the path to God's Kingdom.

Notes

Chapter 1 The Challenge to Christianity in America

1. Most of the data in this book are from surveys conducted by American Resource Bureau. In those surveys, a born-again Christian was defined as someone who:
   1) believes in God;
   2) has made a personal commitment to Jesus Christ that is still important in their life;
   3) believes that they will go to Heaven because Jesus died for their sins, not because of their own merit or any works they have performed during their lifetime.

   Since some of the data are from surveys conducted by other organizations, the definitions occasionally vary, but are generally similar.
2. The primary works used as the foundation for our perspective on the future direction of the nation were:

   Megatrends by John Naisbitt (New York: Warner Books, 1982).

   The Third Wave by Alvin Toffler (New York: Morrow Books, 1980).

   The Winding Passage by Daniel Bell (Cambridge, MA: ABT Associates, 1980).

   New Rules by Daniel Yankelovich (New York: Random House, 1981).
3. "American Values: Change and Stability," *Public Opinion,* December-January 1984, p. 4.

Chapter 2 The American Family Under Change

1. Daniel Yankelovich, *New Rules* (New York: Random House, 1981).
2. *Historical Statistics of the United States, Colonial Times to 1970, Part 1,* U.S. Department of Commerce, Bureau of the Census, 1975, p. 49.

149

3. Statistics provided by U.S. Department of Commerce, Bureau of the Census.
4. Data from American Resource Bureau, Wheaton, IL.
5. "Clergy Divorce Spills into the Aisle," *Christianity Today,* February 5, 1981.
6. Data from American Resource Bureau, Wheaton, IL.
7. *Ibid.*
8. Data provided by Center for Disease Control, Atlanta, GA.
9. *Ibid.*
10. Data from American Resource Bureau, Wheaton, IL.
11. Daniel Yankelovich, *The New Morality* (New York: McGraw-Hill, 1974).
12. *Monitoring the Future,* Institute for Social Research, University of Michigan, reports from 1975-1981, made available through the Roper Center, Storrs, CT.
13. *Who's Who Among American High School Students,* Educational Commission, studies conducted in 1972 and 1979; made available through the Roper Center, Storrs, CT.
14. *Ibid.*

Chapter 3 Educating the Next Generation of Christians

1. This quote, along with other insights into the American education process, were derived from Raymond Moore's book *Homespun Schools.* Dr. Moore's article on home schooling, "The School at Home," which appeared in pp. 18-20 of the March 1984 issue of *Moody Monthly,* presents a brief overview of the topic.
2. Charles Silberman, *Crisis in the Classroom* (New York: Random House, 1970).
3. Based upon information provided by Educational Testing Service, College Entrance Examination Board, Princeton, NJ.
4. *A Decade of Gallup Polls of Attitudes Toward Education,* Stanley Elam, ed., *Phi Delta Kappan,* 1978; "The Fifteenth Annual Gallup Poll of Attitudes Toward the Public Schools," *Phi Delta Kappan,* September 1983.
5. *Ibid.*
6. *Ibid.*
7. In this chapter, a "Christian school" is defined as a school that:
   1) uses a Christ-centered curriculum;
   2) employs born-again Christian teachers and administrators;
   3) consents to an evangelical, Bible-centered statement of faith and practice.
   As such, Catholics schools are excluded from this analysis, as are many schools associated with mainline Protestant denominations.

Notes • 151

8. "Christian Schools Are #2 and Growing," *Journal-ISM,* November 1982, pp. 4-7; "Projections of Student Enrollment in Christian Schools," George Barna and Gregg Quiggle, American Resource Bureau, Wheaton, IL, 1984.
9. Based on data from American Resource Bureau, Wheaton, IL, and the Gallup Organization, Princeton, NJ.
10. "Christian Schools Are #2 and Growing," p. 4; "Projections of Student Enrollment in Christian Schools."
11. Based on data from American Resource Bureau, Wheaton, IL, and the Gallup Organization, Princeton, NJ.
12. "ACSI Students Score Higher than National Average," released by Association of Christian Schools International, 1983.
13. Raymond Moore, "The School at Home," *Moody Monthly,* March 1984, pp. 18-20.
14. Dean Merrill, "Schooling at Mother's Knee," *Christianity Today,* September 2, 1983; interviews with John Whitehead, Rutherford Institute, Manassas, VA, and Raymond Moore, Hewitt Research Institute, Washougal, WA.
15. Data from American Resource Bureau, Wheaton, IL.
16. John Naisbitt, *Megatrends* (New York: Warner Books, 1982).
17. Richard Kriegbaum, "Christian Colleges: Some Will Not Survive," *Christianity Today,* November 12, 1983, pp. 36-39; information from Christian College Coalition, Washington, D.C.
18. "Christian Colleges: Some Will Not Survive," pp. 36-39.
19. Data from American Resource Bureau, Wheaton, IL; information provided by Christian College Coalition, Washington, D.C., National Education Association, Washington, D.C., and Dr. Kenneth Kantzer, Trinity College, Deerfield, IL.
20. Lucia Solorzano and Barbara Quick, "Rating the Colleges," *U.S. News and World Report,* November 28, 1983, pp. 41-48; and data from American Resource Bureau, Wheaton, IL.
21. Data from American Resource Bureau, Wheaton, IL.

Chapter 4 The Media in America

1. For additional information on the impact of the media on our lives see Joseph Klapper, *The Effects of Mass Communication* (New York: Free Press, 1960); Tony Schwartz, *Media: The Second God* (New York: Random House, 1981); Maxwell McCombs and Donald Shaw, "The Agenda-Setting Function of the Mass Media," *Public Opinion Quarterly,* Summer 1972, pp. 176-187; Eli Rubinstein, "Television and Behavior," *American Psychologist,* July 1983, pp. 820-825; Robert MacNeil, *The People Machine* (New York: Harper and Row, 1968).
2. Data from American Resource Bureau, Wheaton, IL.

3. *Statistical Abstract of the United States, 1982,* U.S. Department of Commerce, Bureau of the Census, 1982, p. 555.

4. George Gerbner et al., "The Demonstration of Power: Violence Profile #10," *Journal of Communication,* Summer 1979, pp. 177-196.

5. Albert Bandura and Richard Walters, "Aggression," in *Child Psychology,* Harold Stevenson, ed. (Chicago: University of Chicago Press, 1963), pp. 364-415.

6. National PTA position paper; "The Demonstration of Power: Violence Profile #10," pp. 177-196.

7. "Research on Television Violence and Its Effects on Aggressive Behavior," National PTA, July 1981; *Television and Behavior, Volume 2,* National Institute of Mental Health, 1982; *Television and Growing Up,* U.S. Surgeon General, U.S.G.P.O., 1972.

8. Data from J. Walter Thompson Advertising, New York, NY.

9. *The Gallup Poll Index,* pp. 978-987.

10. Linda Lichter, S. Robert Lichter, and Stanley Rothman, "Hollywood and America: The Odd Couple," *Public Opinion,* January 1983, pp. 54-58.

11. *Ibid.*

12. "Christian Principles Continually Discredited," *NFD Journal,* November-December 1983, p. 13; reports issued by the Federal Communications Division, including Report #5068, Publication #8310-50, News Release #2634, and News Release #46722.

13. Ronald Kaatz, *Cable: An Advertiser's Guide to the New Electronic Media* (Chicago: Crain Books, 1982).

14. *Ibid.;* data from American Resource Bureau, Wheaton, IL.

15. Kenneth Clark, "The Making of a Giant: How Cable Changed America," *Chicago Tribune,* October 30, 1983, Section C, p. 1; data from American Resource Bureau, Wheaton, IL.

16. *Ibid.*

17. Jennifer Bingham Hill, "Subscriber TV Market Seems to Be Fizzling," *Wall Street Journal,* November 23, 1983, p. 29.

18. Data from American Resource Bureau, Wheaton, IL.

19. *Ibid.*

20. *Ibid.*

21. "Cable Competition Continues to Erode Networks' Audience," *Marketing News,* June 10, 1983, p. 3; "New Audience Data Fuel Erosion Debate," *Advertising Age,* July 25, 1983, p. 6; David Bergman, "Poll Shows Most Adults Think TV Quality Down in Past Five Years," *Daily Variety,* June 28, 1983, p. 2.

22. William Martin, "The Birth of a Media Myth," *The Atlantic,* June 1981, pp. 7-16; data from American Resource Bureau, Wheaton, IL.

23. Data from American Resource Bureau, Wheaton, IL.

24. Laura Landro, "United Satellite Seeks $40 Million," *Wall Street Journal,* February 22, 1984, p. 10; Maurine Christopher, "USCI Hunts '85 Funding," *Advertising Age,* February 27, 1984, p. 78; Tom Gerard,

"DBS Makes Its Long-Awaited Bow Today," *Daily Variety,* November 15, 1983, p. 10.

25. Russell Chandler, "Religious Groups Plan Major Use of Video Technology," *Los Angeles Times,* December 25, 1983, Part 1, p. 3.

26. Data from American Resource Bureau, Wheaton, IL.

27. Interview with Michael Clifford, Victory Communications, Phoenix, AZ; interview with spokesman for Oral Roberts Evangelistic Association.

28. Stephen Morin, "Movie Houses Survive Surge in Home Video," *Wall Street Journal,* November 22, 1983, p. 35.

29. S. Robert Lichter and Stanley Rothman, "What Are Moviemakers Made of?", *Public Opinion,* December-January 1984, pp. 14-18.

30. Bernie Whalen, "Illiteracy: The Marketing Research Implications," *Marketing News,* May 13, 1983, pp. 1, 18.

31. Data from American Resource Bureau, Wheaton, IL.

32. "The Folio 400," *Folio,* October 1983, pp. 106, 112, 131, 139; data from American Resource Bureau, Wheaton, IL; "Publication Comparison," *Christian Advertising Forum,* March-April 1984, p. 22.

33. Kenneth Clark, "Norman Lear Takes Another Gamble," *Chicago Tribune,* March 5, 1984, Section 5, pp. 1, 2.

34. Kenneth Clark, "The Making of a Giant: How Cable Changed America," *Chicago Tribune,* October 30, 1983, Tempo section, p. 1.

Chapter 5 Christians in Politics and Community Affairs

1. Alexis de Tocqueville, *Democracy in America* (New York: Washington Square Press, 1971).

2. John Woodbridge, Mark Noll, and Nathan Hatch, *The Gospel in America: Themes in the History of America's Evangelicals* (Grand Rapids, MI: Zondervan, 1979).

3. *Ibid.*

4. Data from the Gallup Organization, Princeton, NJ, poll #AIPO-1160G, available through the Roper Center, Storrs, CT; data from American Resource Bureau, Wheaton, IL.

5. Data from American Resource Bureau, Wheaton, IL.

6. *Ibid.*

7. *Ibid.*

8. *Ibid.*

9. *Ibid.*

10. *Ibid.*

11. Data from the Bureau of the Census, Washington, D.C.

12. Data from the American Resource Bureau, Wheaton, IL.

13. Peter Benson and Dorothy Williams, *Religion on Capitol Hill* (New York: Harper and Row, 1982).

14. *Ibid.*
15. *Ibid.*
16. *Ibid.*
17. *Ibid.*
18. *Ibid.*
19. Based on interviews with spokesmen for National Association of Evangelicals and Congressional staff.
20. Based on a series of articles appearing in *Christianity Today,* 1980-1984.
21. Data from American Resource Bureau, Wheaton, IL.
22. The exhortations found in James 1:22-25 and 2:14-26 are instructive here. For contemporary analyses of how such Scripture can be applied to our lives, consult works such as *Lifestyle in the Eighties,* Ronald Sider, ed. (Philadelphia: Westminster Press, 1982); William Hybels, *Christians in the Marketplace* (Grand Rapids, MI: Zondervan, 1983); and Francis Schaeffer, *A Christian Manifesto* (Westchester, IL: Crossway Books, 1981).
23. Data from American Resource Bureau, Wheaton, IL.

Chapter 6 Personal Spiritual Commitment

1. "Religion in America," the Gallup Organization, Princeton, NJ, 1982; the Gallup Organization, poll #AIP0-1160G, available through the Roper Center, Storrs, CT; "Jesus Christ in the Life of Americans Today," the Gallup Organization, Princeton, NJ, conducted for Robert Schuller Ministries, 1982.
2. *Ibid.*
3. *Ibid.*
4. Data from American Resource Bureau, Wheaton, IL.
5. *Ibid.*
6. *Ibid.*
7. Data from American Resource Bureau, Wheaton, IL, and various surveys made available by the Gallup Organization, Princeton, NJ.
8. "Jesus Christ in the Life of Americans Today," the Gallup Organization, Princeton, NJ, conducted for Robert Schuller Ministries, 1982.
9. Data from the Gallup Organization, Princeton, NJ, poll #USAIPO-SPEC-G077121, available through the Roper Center, Storrs, CT; data from American Resource Bureau, Wheaton, IL.
10. Data from American Resource Bureau, Wheaton, IL.
11. Data made available by the Gallup Organization, Princeton, NJ.
12. *Ibid.*
13. Data from American Resource Bureau, Wheaton, IL; data from Pragmatic Research Applications, Princeton, NJ.
14. Data from American Resource Bureau, Wheaton, IL.
15. *Ibid.*

16. *Ibid.*
17. *Ibid.*

Chapter 7 The Corporate Context of Christianity

1. *The New Bible Dictionary,* J. D. Douglas, ed. (Grand Rapids, MI: Eerdmans, 1979), pp. 228-231.
2. Data from National Council of Churches and World Almanac 1982 (New York: Newspaper Enterprise Association, 1983).
3. Data from American Resource Bureau, Wheaton, IL.
4. *Ibid.*
5. *Understanding Church Growth and Decline,* Dean Hoge and David Roozen, eds. (New York: Pilgrim Press, 1979).
6. Data from American Resource Bureau, Wheaton, IL.
7. *Ibid.*
8. *Ibid.*
9. *Ibid.*
10. Roberta Green, "Cutting Across Convention," *United Evangelical Action,* January-February 1984, pp. 4-7.
11. Data from American Resource Bureau, Wheaton, IL.
12. *Ibid.*
13. Lareta Halteman Finger, "Women in Pulpits," *The Other Side,* July 1979, pp. 14-27.
14. *Ibid.*
15. *Ibid.*
16. Data from American Resource Bureau, Wheaton, IL.

Chapter 8 The Tragedy of Worldliness

1. Etienne Gilson, *The Christian Philosophy of Saint Augustine* (New York: Random House, 1960), pp. 119, 120.
2. M. C. D'Arcy et al., *A Monument to Saint Augustine* (London: Sheed and Ward, 1945), pp. 48-51.
3. Owen Chadwick, *The Reformation* (Grand Rapids, MI: Eerdmans, n.d.), pp. 18, 19.
4. Francis Schaeffer, *A Christian Manifesto* (Westchester, IL: Crossway Books, 1981).
5. Pinnock has written a series of articles in *Christianity Today* since 1982; Sider edited a book entitled *Lifestyle in the Eighties* (Philadelphia: Westminster Press, 1982); Lasch authored *The Culture of Narcissism* (New York: Norton, 1979).
6. Data from American Resource Bureau, Wheaton, IL.